# RUSSIA ACCORDING TO WOMEN

*LITERARY ANTHOLOGY*

Compiled and with a preface by professor

MARINA LEDKOVSKY

HERMITAGE

1991

RUSSIA ACCORDING TO WOMEN
A literary anthology
Compiled and with a preface by Marina Ledkovsky

Copyright (C) 1991 by individual authors and translators

**Library of Congress Cataloging-in-Publication Data**

Rossiia glazami zhenshchin. English
    Russia according to women : literary anthology / compiled and
with a preface by Marina Ledkovsky.
      p. : ill. ; cm.
    Translation of: Rossiia glazami zhenshchin.
    ISBN 1-55779-023-X : $9.50
    1. Russian prose literature--Women authors--Translations into
English. 2. Russian prose literature--20th century--Translations
into English. 3. Soviet Union--Intellectual life--1917- --Literary
collections. I. Ledkovskaia-Astman, Marina. II. Title.
    PG3203.W64R6713    1991
891.78'40808'09287--dc20                        91-11292
                                                        CIP

Photos by Ksana Blank, Tanya Hull, Juni Pierce
Front and back cover photos by Juni Pierce

Published by Hermitage Publishers
P.O. Box 410
Tenafly, N. J. 07670, U.S.A.

# CONTENTS

# FOREWORD

The interest in works by Russian women writers has increased significantly over the past years. The reason for this phenomenon is the emergence of a considerable number of talented female poets and writers whose work renders in a unique literary mode the tragedy of Russian life over the past seven decades. Therefore, it seems especially timely to introduce students of Russian language and culture to Russian women's writings and to their specific understanding of historical events of the latest period. This anthology deals with the entire Soviet period [of Russia's history]. It opens with the memoirs of Anna Akhmatova about her meetings with Aleksandr Blok in 1913-1921, and ends with two sketches by Irina Ratushinskaia, the young poet released from a Soviet prison camp only in late 1986.

The collection includes works by important writers which reflect various aspects of existence in contemporary Russia: family life, work, spiritual quest, human relationship. Tragic motifs are dominant. Before the reader's eyes pass the agonizing and violent break with the great cultural tradition of the past; the fear and humiliation before the tyranny of the new regime; the repression of moral principles and its ugly consequences; the nightmare of arrests, betrayal, prison camps; the absurd housing conditions, the dullness of country life, the mediocrity of health care; women's loneliness in the post-war years; the defenselessness of ordinary small people fallen into disgrace, the alcoholics and those squeezed to the edges of existence or forced into early retirement. Yet, through all those sad themes shine the motifs of love for fellow man, striving for spiritual values, women's readiness for sacrifice, their concern for their loved ones or the

7

misfortunate.

Not coincidentally, five of the included excerpts are drawn from memoirs (Akhmatova, E. Ginzburg, N. Mandel'shtam, Tsvetaeva, L. Chukovskaia). Russian women writers have been successful in this genre for a long time. The first known writing by a Russian woman is, in fact, *Notes Written by Her Own Hand* by Princess Nataliia Borisovna Dolgorukova (1714-1771). Shortly afterward appeared the memoirs of Catherine the Great, Princess Ekaterina Romanovna Dashkova, and in the nineteenth century the *Reminiscences* of Avdot'ia Iakovlevna Panaeva and many others. Memoirs and poetry, genres dealing with intimate and personal experience, seem to have especially attracted feminine talent as they permit the author to depict the world as seen through the prism of her particular perception of existence and its phenomena.

Anna Akhmatova's reminiscences about Blok differ from the following excerpts as they embrace in part the pre-revolutionary period. They are based on Akhmatova's appearance on a televised program on October 12, 1965. She then shared memories of her meetings with Blok in the years 1913-1921. Akhmatova's narrative presents vivid pictures of those "meetings" in remarkably accurate and concise strokes. The last meeting took place shortly before the tragic end of the exhausted poet in the summer of 1921. Akhmatova regarded Blok as "the greatest European poet of the first quarter of the twentieth century." She bitterly mourned his early death.

In the sketch "My [Government] Jobs" Marina Tsvetaeva renders the soul-chilling horror of hunger, cold and War-Communism's overwhelming brutality in her distinctive graphic language. In the narrative's center is the author herself with her perception of the destruction of all that "she had cherished so much." Yet, in spite of all the hardship and the distressing tediousness and uselessness of the "Jobs," Tsvetaeva keeps her humor which at times turns into caustic sarcasm as she observes the new "lifestyle" in the land of the Soviets. Nadezhda Mandel'shtam's as well as Lidiia Chukovskaia's stunning

8

reminiscences are likewise filled with bi\
the authors seem to disappear into the
memories of those most important in their li\ memoirs
    The stories by Ruth Zernova, I. G\cting the
Baranskaia are certainly marked by their own elight.
them, attention is focused on city life, on the Natal'ia
against the incessant odds of everyday exist\es. In
woman's life in the Soviet state. A subtle, m\ruggle
through most works in defiance of the dominant so\ill a
Thus, Liudmila Shtern's story about the "Indestructible\ity. runs
accepted lightly and serenely (in contrast to Venedic\ is
distresing tale on the same theme "Moscow-Petushki"). \'s
    Women have their own distinctive approach to the com\
of existence. Almost always, faith in the victory of Good g\
upper hand over life's nastiness so generously bestowed on the\
fate. Maybe only I. Grekova's and N. Baranskaia's stories ab\
the spiritually bereaved Russian widows of World War II fill th\
reader with sadness until the tales' last lines.
    Of special value is Marina Rachko's heartfelt sketch about
village life in the Russian "nonblack-earth belt." It reveals little
known aspects of the totally destitute way of life of the "masters
of soil and liberty." In those impassable backwoods people quench
their thirst for spiritual values with abundant alcohol to suppress
the realization of their impasse. Yet, their thirst is unquenchable
and Rachko know how to convince her readers of this calamity.
    The gifted Bella Akhmadulina is aptly represented by an
excerpt from her novella published in the almanac *Metropol'* in
1979. (This almanac was not permitted to appear in the Soviet
Union; it was published by Ardis Publishers in the U.S.A.) Clever
shifts in time and space sequences, impregnated with philosophical
thought, connect her prose with the best contemporary innovative
writing. Likewise, the excerpt from a *samizdat* novella
"Leningrad-Tbilisi" is quite engaging. Its author, T. Nikolaeva (a
pseudonym), belonged to a group of "unofficial" writers at the time
of the story's appearance. The excerpt's action takes place in the
late 1970's and introduces the reader to the much more liberal

9

rrelationship seems to be more
...at one gains the impression that
empire "man indeed can breathe
...ushinskaia's two sketches return the
...nce in which the human soul has to

the images of women "do not enjoy any
...y are depicted realistically, without ideal-
...out the opposite extreme – the singling out of
...part of the human race.

...arranged in chronological order, from 1913 to
...the hope of enhancing the collection's value as a
...inner slice of Russia's newest history. Despite the
...y of themes – city dwelling, burearcracy, the literary
...spitals, village life, etc. – a sense of unity pervades the
...because of the inconspicuous presence of that intimate
aime intonation discussed earlier. For that reason it should
...eal not only to students of Russian, but to every reader who is
...t indifferent to the culture, history and fate of Russia.

**Marina Ledkovsky**
*Barnard College*
*Columbia University*

Anna Akhmatova


# MEMORIES OF A. BLOK



In St. Petersburg in the autumn of 1913, on the day of a celebration at some restaurant in honor of the visiting Verkharn, there was a big students-only party at the Bestuzhevskii Women's College. One of the hostesses got it into her head to invite me. So, in store for me was an evening of honoring Verkharn, whom I loved tenderly not for his famed urbanism, but for one little poem: "On a Little Wooden Bridge at the Edge of the World."

But I pictured a magnificent St. Petersburg restaurant feast, which for some reason always resembled a funeral banquet: evening dresses and coat-tails, good champagne, and bad French, and toasts. And frankly I preferred the students.

On this particular evening the lady patrons who had dedicated their lives to women's rights had come. One of them, writer Ariadna Vladimirovna Tyrkova-Vergezhskaia, who had known me since childhood, said after my reading, "Now Anichka here has secured equality of rights for herself."

In the green-room I bumped into Blok.

I asked him why he wasn't at the dinner honoring Verkharn. The poet answered with touching straightforwardness, "Because there they'll ask me to perform and I don't speak French."

A student with a list came over to us and informed me that I was scheduled to read after Blok. I implored him, "Aleksandr Aleksandrovich, I can't perform after you." He reproachfully replied, "Anna Andreevna, we are not tenors." At this time he was already one of the most famous poets in Russia. I had already been reading my works for two years relatively frequently at the Poets' Guild, the Society of Admirers of the Artistic Word and Viacheslav Ivanov's Tower, but this was altogether different.

11

As much as a stage hides a man, a podium mercilessly exposes him. It is . . . something like an executioner's block. It was at that moment, perhaps, that I truly felt that for the first time. It seems to the performer that all present begin to form some sort of multi-headed hydra. Being master of the audience is a very difficult business — Zoschenko was a master; Pasternak, too.

No one knew me, and when I stepped out a cry was heard: "Who's this?" Blok advised me to read "All you drunkards . . ." I started to refuse, "When I read 'I Donned a Narrow Skirt,' they laugh." He replied, "When I read 'And Rabbit-Eyed Drunkards' they laugh too."

I think that, not there, but at some other literary gathering, Blok was listening to Igor Severianin. He came back to the green-room and said, "He has the greasy voice of a lawyer."

On one of the last Sundays of '13, I brought Blok his books, so he could autograph them. On each he wrote simply, "For Akhmatova — Blok." Here's *Poems of a Wonderful Lady.* On the third volume he wrote me a madrigal, "Beauty is frightening, they'll tell you . . ." I'd never had a Spanish shawl like the one in which I'm portrayed in the poem, but at the time Blok was infatuated with Carmen and Spanish-ized even me. I, of course, never wore a red rose in my hair either. It's not by accident that that poem is written as a romancer's Spanish stanza. At our last meeting, backstage at the Great Dramatic Theater, in the spring of 1921, Blok came up to me and asked, "Where's the Spanish shawl?" Those were the last words I ever heard from him.

\* \* \*

The single time that I was at Blok's, I actually mentioned to him that the poet Benedict Livshits jokes that his ability to write poetry is hindered by Blok's very existence. Blok didn't laugh, but answered completely seriously, "I understand that. My ability to write is hindered by Leo Tolstoy."

12

In the summer of 1914 I was at my mother's in Darnitsa, outside of Kiev. In early July I went home to Slepnev Village through Moscow. In Moscow, I get on the first mail train I see. I'm smoking on the open landing at the end of the caboose. Somewhere, at some deserted platform, a train stops, and a bagful of letters is thrown inside it. In front of my bewildered eyes, suddenly Blok appears. I yell, "Aleksandr Aleksandrovich!" He looks around and, as he was not only a great poet, but also a master of tactful questions, asks, "With whom are you traveling?" I have time to answer, "Alone." The train is off.

Today, 51 years later, I open Blok's notebook and under July 9, 1914 I read, "Mom and I went to look at the sanatorium beyond Podsolnechnoia. – The demon teases me. – Anna Akhmatova on a mail train."

Blok writes in another place how Del'mas, E.I. Kuz'mina-Karavaeva and I tortured him over the phone. It seems that I can provide some information on the subject.

I called Blok. Aleksandr Aleksandrovich with his characteristic straightforwardness and habit of thinking aloud asks, "You are, probably, calling because Ariadna Vladimirovna Tyrkova told you what I said about you?" Dying of curiosity, I went to Ariadna Vladimirovna's house on some reception day of hers and asked what Blok had said. But she was implacable: "Anichka, I never tell one of my guests what was said about her by another."

Blok's *Notebook* presents many small gifts, evoking oblivion from the abyss and returning dates to half-forgotten events. Once again: the wooden St. Isaac's Bridge, flaming, swims toward the mouth of the Neva, and my traveling companion and I stare in horror at this unprecedented sight, and this day has a date – July 11, 1916, noted by Blok.

And once again: I, already after the Revolution (January 21, 1919), meet the emaciated Blok, his eyes mad, in a theater cafeteria and he says to me, "Everyone runs into each other here, like in the other world."

Oh, and here's where the three of us (Blok, Gumilev and I) are dining (August 5, 1914) on the Tsarskosel'skii train during the first days of the war (Gumilev is in uniform). Blok at this time is going around to the families of the mobilized soldiers to render his assistance. When we were alone, Kolia said, "Is it really possible that they would send even him to the front? Why, that's like roasting nightingales."

And after a quarter century, at the one and the same Dramatic Theater — an evening in memory of Blok (1946), and I'm reading only poetry written by me:

> He's right — again streetlight, drugstore,
> Neva, silence, granite . . .
> Like a monument to the beginning of the century,
> There stands this man —
> When to Pushkin's house,
> In saying good bye, he waved his hand
> And accepted death's langour
> Like an undeserved peace.

October, 1965

*Translated by Natasha Yefimov*

Marina Tsvetaeva

# MY JOBS

November 15th, the third day of my job.
I'm compiling an archive of newspaper clippings. That is: I recapitulate Steklov, Kerzhentsev, accounts about prisoners of war, the movements of the Red Army, and so forth, in my own words. I recapitulate once, I recapitulate twice (I copy from the "journal of newspaper clippings" onto "cards"), then I glue these clippings onto enormous sheets. The newspapers are delicate, the type barely noticeable, and then add captions in lilac pencil, and then the glue — it's utterly pointless and will return to ashes even before it's all burned.

There are different desks here: Estonian, Latvian, Finnish, Moldavian, Moslem, Jewish and several entirely inarticulate ones. In the morning each desk receives its share of clippings, which it then processes over the course of the day. I see all this clipping, labeling and pasting as endless, convoluted variations on one and the same, very meager, theme. As though a composer only had it in him to invent one musical phrase, and he had to fill about thirty reams of musical notation paper — so he variates: and we variate.

I forgot to mention the Polish and Bessarabian desks. I, not without justification, am the "Russian" desk (the assistant of the secretary, or perhaps of the director).

Each desk — is grotesque.

To my left — two dirty, doleful Jewesses, ageless, like herring. Further on: a red, fair-haired Latvian woman — also frightening, like a person turned into a sausage: "I knew khim, such a sveetie. Khe partissipated in ze plot, und now zey haf zentenced khim to be shot. Chik-chik". . . And she giggles with excitement. Wears a red shawl. The fat, bright pink display of her neck.

The Jewess says: "Pskov is taken!" I have the tormenting

15

thought: "By whom?!!"

Only later did I understand: "taken" — is of course: "by us!" If it were the Whites — then it would be: "given up."

To my right — two people (the Oriental table). One has a nose and no chin, the other has a chin and no nose. (Who is Abkhazia and who is Azerbaijan?).

Behind me is a seventeen–year–old child — pink, healthy, curly–headed (a white Negro), easy–thinking and easy–loving, a real live Atenais from Anatole France's "The Gods Thirst". [. . .]

Also — a type of institute class–supervisor lady ("an inveterate theatergoer"), also — a greasy, obese Armenian woman (chin resting on chest, impossible to say what's where), a half–breed in student uniform, also an Estonian doctor, sleepy and a born drunk. . . . Also (variety!) a doleful Latvian woman, all drained out. Also. . . .[. . . ]

* * *

An encounter.

I'm running to the Commissariat. Supposed to be there at nine — it's already eleven: I stood on line for milk on Kudrinskaia St., for salted fish at Povarskaia, for hemp–seed oil on the Arbat.

There's a lady in front of me: ragged, skinny, with a bag. I come up alongside her. The bag is heavy, her shoulder bowed, I feel the tension of the arms.

"Excuse me ma'am. May I help you?"

Frightened flight:

"Oh, no. . . ."

"I'd be glad to carry it, don't worry, we'll walk together."

She gives in. The bag really is hellish.

"Do you have far to go?"

"To Butyrki, I'm bringing a package."

"Has he been in long?"

"Quite a few months."

"No one to vouch?"

"All Moscow would vouch for him — that's why they won't let him out."

"Young?"

"No, middle-aged. . . ."

"Your father died?"

"Before the war."

"You don't know anymore, whether to be sorry or envious."

"Live. And try to keep others alive. God be with you!"

"Thank you. The same to you."


\*   \*   \*


The Institute.

Did I ever think that after so many schools, boarding schools and gymnasiums, I would be handed over to an Institute as well?! For I'm in an Institute, and have in fact been handed over (by X). I arrive between 11 and 12 o'clock; each time my heart stands still: the Director and I have the same habits (ministerial ones!). I'm talking about the head Director – M-ra, my own personal director, Ivanov, I write with a small letter.

Once we met at the coat rack – it was all right. A Pole: courteous. And then I'm also Polish on my grandmother's side.

But more terrifying than the Director – are the doormen. The former ones. They seem disdainful. In any case, they don't greet you first, and I'm shy. After the doormen, the main worry is not to mix up the rooms. (My idiocy for places.) I'm ashamed to ask, it's my second month here. Enormous idols stand in the hall – knights-in-armor. Left for their uslessness . . . to everyone but me. But I need them, just as I alone of everyone here, am akin to them. I ask for protection with a glance. From beneath their visors they answer. If no one's watching, I quietly stroke a forged leg. (Three times taller than I.)

The hall.

I enter, awkward and timid. In a mousey man's jersey – like a mouse. I'm dressed worse then everyone here, and that's not reassuring. Shoes tied with strings. There may even be some shoe laces somewhere, but . . . who needs it?

The main thing is: to understand from the first second of the Revolution: All is lost! Then – all is easy.

I steal by. The director (my own, the small one) – from his seat:

"Were you waiting in line comrade Efron?" "In three lines." "What did they have?" "They didn't have anything, they had salt." "Yes, well, salt sure isn't sugar!"

Heaps of clippings. Some are quite long, some only a line. I look for ones about the White Guards. The pen scratches. The stove crackles.

"Comrade Efron, we have horse meat for lunch today. I suggest you sign up."

"No money. Did you sign up?"

"Certainly not!"

"Well then, we'll drink tea. Shall I bring you some?"

* * *

The corridors are empty and clean. The click of typewriters behind doors. Pink walls, columns and snow in the windows. My noble, pink, paradise Institute! Wandering about, I come upon the descent to the kitchen: the descent of the Virgin into hell or of Orpheus into Hades. Stone tiles, worn by human feet. Sloping, nothing to hold on to, the steps twist and turn, in one place they fly headlong. Those peasant legs certainly did their work! And to think, in indoor, homemade shoes! It's as though they've been gnawed by teeth. Yes, the tooth of the only old man with any bite! The tooth of Chronos!

Natasha Rostova! Did you ever walk here? My ballroom Psyche! Why wasn't it you — later, at some point — who met Pushkin? Even the name is the same! Literary historians wouldn't have had to relearn anything. Pushkin — instead of Pierre, and Parnassus — instead of nappies. To become a fertility goddess, having been Psyche — Natasha Rostova — isn't that a sin?

It would have been like this. He would have come to call. Having heard so much about the poet and Arab, you would have turned your pointed, bright-eyed little face up — and laughing at something, already feeling a pang. . . . Oh, the flounce of a pink gown against the column!

The column overflows with heavenly foam! And your — Aphrodite's, Natasha's, Psyche's — lyrical foot on the slippery peasant stones.

Actually, you were only flying down them to the kitchen for bread!

But everything comes to an end: Natasha, serfdom and the

18

staircase (they say eventually, even Time!). By the way, the stairs are not that long — only twenty-two steps in all. It's only that I walked down them for so long (1818 – 1918).

Firm. (I almost said: firmament. I was younger and there was the monarchy — and I didn't understand: why the *heavenly* firmament. The revolution and my own soul have taught me). Pot-holes, pitfalls, cave-ins. Groping hands grip wet walls. Close over my head, the vault. It smells of damp and Bonivard. Methinks chains are clanking. Ach, no, it's the clang of pots and pans from the kitchen! I go toward the lantern.

The kitchen is a crater. So red and hot it's obvious: Hell. A huge, six and a half meter stove spews forth fire and foam. "The seething cauldrons boil, they sharpen their knives of steel, they ready the goat for slaughter." . . . And I am the goat.

The queue for the kettle. They scoop ladlefuls straight from the boiler. The tea is wood-pulp, some say from bark, others from buds, I just lie — from roots. Not glass — but a burn. I pour two glasses. I wrap them in a flap of jersey. On the threshold I inhale horse-flesh with a slight movement of the nostrils: I can't sit here — I have no friends.

"Well then, comrade Efron, now we can goof off a bit!"
(I've arrived with the glasses).
"With saccharine or without?"
"Pour on the saccharine!"
"They say it affects your kidneys. But you know, I . . . ."
"Yes, you know, I too . . . ."
My director is an esperantist (that is, a communist from Philology). An esperantist from Ryazan. When he talks about Esperanto a quiet madness glimmers in his eyes. The eyes are light and small, like the ancient saints', or like Pan in the Tretiakov Gallery. See-through. A touch of the lecher. But not the lechery of the flesh, some other kind — it weren't for the absurdity of the association I'd say: other-wordly. (If it's possible to love Eternity, then it's also possible to lust after her! And the lusters (philologists) are more numerous than the silent lovers!)

Dark blonde. Something in the nose and chin. The face is puffy, groggy. A drunkard, I imagine.

He writes in the new style – in anticipation of world-wide esperanto. Has no political convictions. Here, where everyone's a communist, even this is a blessing. Doesn't distinguish reds from whites. Doesn't distinguish right from left. Doesn't distinguish men from women. For this reason his comradery is completely sincere, and I willingly pay him with the same coin. After work he goes somewhere on Tverskaia, where on the left side (if you're heading down toward Okhotny) there's an esperanto store. They closed the store, the storefront window remained: fly-blown postcards esperantists have sent each other from all corners of the earth. He looks and lusts. He works here because it offers an enlarged field for propaganda: all nations. But he's already beginning to despair.

"I'm afraid, comrade Efron, that here there are more and more . . . (in a whisper) kikes, kikes and Latvians. It wasn't even worth applying: Moscow's full of these goods! I was counting on Chinese, on Indians. They say that Indians readily digest foreign cultures."

I: "Not Hindus – American Indians."

He: "Redskins?"

I: "That's right, with feathers. They'll slit your throat – and digest you in one piece. If you're wearing a jacket, then jacket and all, in a tuxedo – tuxedo and all. But Hindus – just the opposite: terribly dense. Won't swallow anything foreign, neither ideology nor foodstuffs. (Becoming inspired): – Do you want a formula? The American Indian digests (the European), the Indian disgorges (Europe). And rightly so."

He, embarrassed: "Now, really, you're . . . I, by the way . . . I've heard more from the communists, they are *also* counting on India . . . (Becoming inspired in his turn): I'd thought – I'll up and esperanto them all! (Subsiding): – No rations – and not one Indian. Not one Negro! Not even a Chinaman! . . . And these (a circular glance at the empty hall) – don't want to hear of it! I tell them: Esperanto, and they say: the International! (Frightened by his own cry): I've nothing against it, but first Esperanto, and then . . . . The *word* first . . ."

I, falling in: "And then the *deed*. Of course. In the beginning was the word and the word was. . . ."

He, in another outburst: "And that Mara-Mara! What is it? Where did they get it from? Not only haven't I heard a word from him: I haven't heard a sound! He's just a deaf mute. Or an idiot. Doesn't receive any clippings — only his salary. I don't begrudge it. To hell with him, but *why does he come?* The fool, he comes every day. Sits here till four, the fool. He should just come on the 20th, for pay-day.

I, craftily: "Poor thing, maybe he keeps hoping? I'll come and on my desk there'll be a newspaper cutting about my Mara-Mara?"

He, irritated: "Ach, comrade Efron, really! What cuttings? Who's going to write about that Mara-Mara? Where is it? What is it? Who needs it?"

I, thoughtfully: "It isn't in geography. . . . (Pause). And it isn't in history. . . . What if it doesn't exist at all? They just invented it — to show off. You know, all nations. And they dressed this guy up. . . . But he's mute (confidentially): they chose a deaf mute on purpose, so he wouldn't give himself away in Russian. . . ."

He, gulping the last bit of cold tea with a shudder:

"Who the dddevil knows!"


Clatter and crash. It's all the nationalities returning from their feed. Fortified with horse-flesh, it's on to the cutting files (on to filet cutlets would be better, eh? By the way, before the revolution, cross my heart, I not only couldn't tell filet from tripe — I couldn't tell groats from flour! And I don't regret it in the least).

Comrade Ivanov, anxiously: "Comrade Efron, comrade M-r might drop in, let's get rid of our mess quickly, eh? (He rakes it in.): "The Red Army's Advance" . . . Steklov's articles . . . "The Liquidation of Illiteracy" . . . . "Down with the White Guard Scum" — That's for you. "The Bourgeoisie Schemes" . . . You again . . . "All to the Red Front" . . . Mine . . . "Trotsky's Address to the Troops" . . . Mine . . . "The White Hoarders and the White Guard" . . . Yours . . . "Kolchak's Lackeys" . . . Yours . . . "The Whites' Atrocities" . . . Yours . . .

I'm drowning in whiteness. At my elbow — Mamontov, on my knees — Denikin, near my heart — Kolchak.

Greetings, my "White Guard Scum!"

I write with relish.

"What's going on comrade Efron, why haven't you finished? The paper, no., date, who, what — no details! I was that way at first too — filled sheets full, then M-r admonished me: you're using up a lot of paper.

"Does M-r believe in it?"

"What's to believe! You copy, you clip, you glue. . . ."
"And into the Lethe — boom! Like in Pushkin."
"Yes, but M–r's a very educated person, I still haven't lost hope. . . ."
"You don't say! I thought so too. I ran into him not long ago at the hangings . . . ach, good Lord . . . at the coat hangers: I've got all these "White Guard Atrocities" in my head. . . . A quarter past twelve! It was all right, he even looked at me rather intelligently. . . . So, you have hope?"
"Somehow I'll manage to get him to the esperanto club one of these evenings."[. . . ]


"Comrade Efron! (A whisper almost in my ear.) I jump. My "white negro" is standing behind me and she's all red. There's bread in her hand.
"You didn't have lunch, perhaps you'd like it? Only I warn you, it's made with bran. . . ."
"But you yourself, I'm so embarrassed. . . ."
"Do you think . . . (an ardent face, a challenge in every sheep's curl) . . . I bought it at Smolensky? Filimovich from the Eastern desk gave it to me — it's his rations, he doesn't eat it himself. I ate half, half's for you. He promised more tomorrow. But I still won't kiss him!" [. . .]

Don — Don. — Not the river Don, a ringing gong. Two o'clock. And — a further illumination: I'll think up some emergency and I'll leave right away. I'll finish up the White Guards — and I'll leave. Quickly and without any more lyrical digressions (I myself — am just such a digression!) I shower the grey official paper with the pearls of my script and the vipers of my heart. But that counterrevolutionary yat' keeps popping up, like a church cupola. — Yat'!!! — "Comrade Kerzhentsev ends his article by wishing General Denikin a good and speedy hanging: we, in turn, wish the same for comrade Kerzhentsev. . . ."
"Saccharine! Saccharine! They're signing up for saccharine!" Everyone jumps up. I must take advantage of other people's sweet cravings to satisfy my own freedom craving. Ingratiatingly and impudently I slip Ivanov my clippings. I cover them with half of the

white negro's bread. (The other half is for the children.)

"Comrade Ivanov, I'm leaving now. If M–r asks, say that I'm in the kitchen getting a drink of water."

"Go on, go on."

I rake up the draft of Casanova, a purse with a pound of salt . . . and sidling, sidling. . . .

"Comrade Efron!" – he catches up with me near the knights. "I won't be coming at all tomorrow. I'd really appreciate it if you'd come – well – at least by 10:30. And then the day after tomorrow, don't come at all. You'll really help me out. All right?"

"Yes sir!"

There and then, in front of the perplexed doormen, I salute dashingly and rush – rush through the White Guard colonnade, over the snowy flowerbed, leaving behind me nationalities and saccharine and esperanto and Natasha Rostova – to my house, to Alya, to Casanova: homeward! [. . .]


*  *  *


In our Narkomnats there's a private chapel – Sollogub's, of course. Near my pink hall. The "white negro" and I stole in there not long ago. Dark, sparkling, cellar air. We stood in the choir gallery. The "white negro' crossed herself, but I was thinking more about ancestors (ghosts). In church I feel like praying only when they sing. But I don't feel God inside places at all.

Love – and God. How do they sing it? (Love as the element of loving, the earthly Eros). I glance at my white negro: she's praying; innocent eyes. The very same innocent eyes, the same praying lips. . . .

If I were a believer and loved men, this would all fight inside of me like chained dogs.

My "white negro's" father works as a doorman in one of the (palaces) where Lenin often comes (the Kremlin). And my "white negro," who is often at work with her father, sees Lenin all the time. – "So humble, he wears a cap."

My white negro – is a white guard, that is, not to confuse things: she loves white flour, sugar and all earthly blessings. And what's even more serious, she is passionately and profoundly devout.

"He walks by me, M.I., and I say 'Good day Vladimir Ilich!' – while myself (a bold-cautious look around): Ach, I'd like to shoot you right now, you so and so, with a revolver. Don't rob churches! (Flaring up). And you know, M.I., it would be so simple – pull a revolver out of my muff and finish him off! . . . (Pause.) Only I don't know how to shoot, you see. . . . And they'd shoot Papa."

If my negro were to fall into the right hands, hands that know how to shoot and how to teach shooting, and, more important, that know how to destroy and know no regret – e-ekh! [. . .]

But there's another one – plump, raw, a grandmother's granddaughter, girlfriend of my white negro, a provincial lass. A very poignant little girl. She arrived only recently from Rybinsk. Grandmother and brother remain at home. A two-fold, inexhaustible mine of bliss.

"That's just the way our grandmother is: she can't stand little children. She won't go near an infant: they smell, she says, and they're trouble. But when they get bigger – well, all right then. She'll dress them, teach them. Me she raised from the age of six. – 'Do you want to eat? – Yes. – Well, then, go to the kitchen and watch how dinner's made.' – So by ten I already knew how to do absolutely everything (animatedly): not just your meat pies and cutlets – pâté and aspics and cakes. . . . The same for sewing: 'You, little one, you'll be a woman one day, a housewife, with children and a husband to sew for.' I'd want to run around, she takes my hand and sits me down on the bench: 'hem those kerchiefs,' 'embroider those towels,' and when the war started – for the wounded. Cut patterns herself, sewed herself. Then Papa got married – I'm an orphan – little brother came along, she made his whole layette herself. . . . All the diapers with embroidered initials, with satin-stitch. . . . And his little blanket, clothes to take him out in, all sewn with my lace, four-fingers wide, cream-colored. . . . (Blissfully): You know, grandmother taught me to knit and satin-stitch. . . . She ordered me my own embroidery hoop. We lived well! And she did everything by herself! Grandmother made things herself, I make things myself. . . . I can't stand for my hands to lie idle!"

I look at her hands! Golden hands! Small, plump; slender, tapered fingers. A tiny ring with a tiny turquoise. There was a fiancé, shot by the firing squad not long ago in Kiev.

24

"His friend wrote to me, he's a student too — a medical student. My Kolia leaves the house, hasn't gone two feet — shots ring out. And a man falls right at his feet. All bloody. And Kolia's — a doctor, he can't leave someone who's wounded. He looked around: nobody. So he took him, dragged him into his own house and looked after him for three days. He turned out to be a white officer. And on the fourth day they came, took them both, and shot them together. . . ."

She dresses in mourning. Her face a sallow grey amid the blackness. Not enough food, not enough sleep, loneliness. Tedious, incomprehensible, unaccustomed work in the Commissariat. Her fiancé's ghost. Homelessness.

Poor Turgenevian petite bourgeoise! The epic orphan of Russian fairytales! In no one do I feel the great orphanhood of Moscow 1919 as I do in her. Not even in myself.

She dropped by to see me recently, stood over my disarrayed trunks: a student uniform, officer's jacket, boots, riding breeches — epaulets, epaulets, epaulets. . . .

"Marina Ivanovna, you should shut them. Shut them and put a lock on. Dust builds up, moths will eat them in the summer . . . He might still return. . . ."

And, pensively smoothing a helpless sleeve:

"I couldn't. Just like a live person. . . . I'm crying now. . . ."

\* \* \*

We migrate to another campfire — from the Rostov's house to the Jerusalem townhouse. It takes a whole ten days to sort ourselves out. We make off with the remains of the Rostov- Sollogub goods. I took a plate with a coat of arms as a souvenir. In a brick-red field — a borzoi. A lyrical theft, even chivalrous: the plate isn't deep or small, in this day and age — it's obviously for salted fish stew, but in my home the inkwell will stand in it.

Those poor Sollogubian Elzevirs! In open boxes! In the rain! Parchment bindings, ornate French type. . . . They carry them away by the cartloads. The library commission is headed by Briusov.

They take away: sofas, chests of drawers, chandeliers. My knights remain. So do the portraits painted on the wall, it seems. Right on the spot — the divvy. The jealous dispute of the "desks."

"That's for our director!"

"No, for our's."

"We already have the Karelian birch table, and the armchair goes with it."

"That's precisely why, you have the table, we get the armchair."

"But you can't break the set!"

I, sententiously:

"Only heads can be broken!"

The 'desks" are disinterested – we won't get anything anyway. Everything goes into the directors' offices. In flies my white negro:

"Comrade Efron! If you only knew how wonderful it is at Ts–ler's! A redwood secretary, a rug, bronze sconces! Just like in the old days! Do you want to take a look?"

We run through the floors. Room No. . . . Section such and such. . . . The director's office. We enter. My negro, triumphantly:

"Well?"

"Just add a cushion under foot and a lapdog. . . ."

"A cat would be enough!"

In her eyes, a joyful demon.

"Comrade Efron! Let's catch him a cat! There's one in apartment 18. What do you say?"

I, hypocritically:

"But he'll dirty everything here."

"That's exactly what I want! Darn thugs!"

Three minutes later the cat is nabbed and shut in. "Work" is over. We fly down all six flights, forgetting everything.

"Comrade Efron! The raspberry ottoman, eh?"

"And the countess's rugs, no?"

The diabolic meowing of the avenger pursues us. [. . .]


*  *  *


Frozen potatoes.

"Comrade Efron! They've brought potatoes! Frozen!"

I, of course, find out later than everyone, but bad news – always too soon.

Some of "our people" went on an expedition, promised sugar mines and lodes of fat, traveled about for two months and brought back . . . frozen potatoes! Three poods a head. First thought: how to get them home? Second: how to eat them? The three poods were rotting.

The potatoes are in the cellar, in a deep, pitch-dark crypt. The potatoes gave up the ghost and were buried, and we, the jackals, are going to dig them up and eat them. They say they arrived healthy, but then someone suddenly "prohibited" them, and by the time the prohibition was lifted, the potatoes, having first frozen and then thawed out, had rotted. They sat at the train station for three weeks.

I run home for sacks and the sled. The sled – is Alya's, a child's sled with little bells and blue reins – my gift fo her from Rostov in the Vladimir region. Spacious wicker-work like they use for baskets, the back upholstered with a handmade rug. Just harness two dogs – and mush! – off to the Northern Lights. . . .

But it was I who served as the dog, and the northern lights stayed behind: her eyes! She was two years old then, and she was regal. ("Marina, give me the Kremlin!" pointing at the towers.) Ach, Alya! Ach, the sled along midday lanes! My little tiger-fur coat (baltic leopard? snow leopard?) which Mandelstam, having fallen in love with Moscow, stubbornly designated Boyaresque. Snow leopard! Sleigh bells!

There's a long line to the cellar. The frost-bitten steps of the staircase. Cold at your back: how to lug them? My hands – I believe in these marvels, but 100 pounds upstairs! Up thirty leaning, pushing steps! Besides which, one of the runners is broken. Besides which, I'm not sure the sacks will hold. Besides all of which, I'm enjoying myself so much that – even if I died – no one would help.

They let us in groups: ten at a time. Everyone's in pairs – husbands have run over from their jobs. Mothers have dragged over. Lively negotiations, plans: one will exchange, another will dry two poods, a third will put them through the meat grinder (100 pounds?!) – obviously, I am the only one who intends to *eat* them.

"Comrade Efron, are you going to take the supplement? A half-pood for every family member. Do you have a certificate for the children?"

Someone:

"I wouldn't! There's only slime left."

Someone else:

"You can unload it!"

We forge ahead. Grunts and sighs, occasionally laughter: someone's hands have met in the darkness: men's and women's (men's and men's – isn't funny). Apropos, whence this jollying effect of Eros on the simple people? Defiance? Self-defense? Impoverished means of expression? Timidity under the guise of levity. After all, when they're afraid, children often laugh as well. [. . .]

– But maybe – more likely – no amour, just surprise: men's hands – curses, a man's and a woman's – laughter. Surprise and impunity.

There's talk of an impending trial for the coworkers – they presented huge bills for both purchases and expenses. Some lodging, supplies carts, drivers. . . .

Themselves, of course, they supplied with everything.

"Did you notice how so and so's fattened up?"

"And so and so? His cheeks are about to burst!"

They let us in. We run into a crazed string of sleds. Runners over feet. Shouts. Darkness. We go through puddles. The smell is truly putrid.

"Move aside, will you!!!"

"Comrades! Comrades! The bag broke!"

Squish. Squelch. The feet disappear up to the ankles. Someone, braking the entire team, furiously removes his footwear: his felt boots are soaked through! I stopped feeling my feet a long time ago.

"Hey! Is there ever going to be any light?!"

"Comrades! I lost my identification! In the name of all that's holy – light a match!"

It sputters. Someone on their knees, in the water, is helplessly raking aside the slime.

"You should look in your pockets!" "Could you have left it at home?"

"How do you think you'll find it here?" "Move along! Move along!"

"Comrades, there's another group coming this way! Watch out!!!"

And – a glade and a waterfall. A square hole in the ceiling, through which rain and light fall. It gushes, as if from a dozen pipes. – We'll drown! – Leaps and jumps, someone lost their sack, someone else's sled got stuck in the passageway. – Lord Almighty!

The potatoes are on the floor: they took up three hallways. At the far end they're more protected, less rotten. But there's no way to get to them except over them. And so: with our feet, our boots. Like climbing over a mountain of jellyfish. You have to take them with your hands: one hundred pounds. The unthawed ones have stuck together in monstrous clusters. I don't have a knife. So, in despair (I can't feel my hands) — I grab whatever kind comes my way: squashed, frozen, thawed. . . . The sack won't hold any more. My hands, numb through and through, can't tie it. Taking advantage of the darkness, I start to cry, but there and then I stop:

"To the scales! To the scales! Who's ready for the scales?!"

I hoist and haul.

Two Armenians are doing the weighing, one in a student uniform, the other in Caucasian dress. The snow-white felt cloak looks like a spotted hyena. Just like an archangel of the Communist Last Judgment! (The scales undoubtedly lie!)

"Comrrrade Meess! Don't hold up the public!"

Quarreling, kicking. Those in back push. I've blocked the entire passageway. Finally, the Caucasian, taking pity — or growing angry, shoves my sack aside with his foot. Poorly tied, the sack spills open. Slip. Slobber. I gather them up patiently, taking my time.


The return route with the potatoes. (I only took two poods, the third I stashed away.) First through raging hallways, then along a resisitant stairway — whether it's tears or sweat on my face I can't tell,

> And I know not whether it be tears or rain
> That burn my face. . . .

Maybe it was rain! That's not the point! The runner is very weak, it's split in the middle, it's unlikely we'll make it back. (It's not I who pulls the sled, we pull together. The sled — is my comrade-in-woe, and the potatoes — are the woe. We carry our own woe!)

I'm scared of the plazas. Arbat can't be avoided. I could have gone by thePrechistenka lanes, but would have gotten lost there. Neither snow, nor ice: I'm sliding on water, and in some places — on dry ground. I admire the cobblestones pensively, some are already pink. . . .

"Oh how I loved all this!"

I remember Stakhovich. If he were to see me now, I would unavoidably become the object of his loathing. Everything, even my face, is dripping. I am no better than my own sack. The potatoes and I are now one and the same.

29

"Where the hellrya goin? Canya like that — right into people?! Tailess bourgeoise!"
"Of course I've no tail — only devils have tails!"
Laughter all around. The soldier, not assuaged:
"Some hat yur decked out in! And that mug could use a washing. . . ."
I, in the same tone, pointing to his leg-wrappings:
"Some rags you're decked out in!"
The laughter grows. Not wanting to relinquish the dialogue, I stop, and pretend to adjust the sack.
The soldier, working himself up:
"The upper classes they call 'em! Hah! Intellygents! Can't wash our face without a servant, can we?!"
A simple woman, shrilly:
"You'll give her some soap then, will you? Who's slipped off with all the soap, tell me? What's soap going for at Sukhareva, d'ya know?"
Someone from the crowd:
"How would he know? He gets it for free! And you, Miss, you've got potatoes there?"
"Frozen. From my job."
"Of course they're frozen — they need the good ones for themselves! Give you a hand, then?"
He gives a push, the reins strain, I'm off. Behind me the woman's voice — to the soldier:
"So what, she wears a hat, so she's not a human being?
The ver-dict!

The day's outcome: two tubs of potatoes. We all eat: Alya, Nadia, Irina, I.
Nadia — to Irina, slyly:
"Eat, Irina, it's sweet, with sugar."
Irina, stubbornly, lowering her head: "Nnnnnoooo. . . ." [. . .]

\* \* \*


April 25, 1919.
I quit Comissariat. I quit because I can't put together a classification. I tried, I rackes my brains — zilch. I *don't* understand. I don't understand what they want from me:"Compile, compare,

30

sort. . . . In each section — a subsection." As if they'd rehearsed. I asked everyone: from the department director to the eleven-year-old messenger boy. "It's very simple."

And the main thing is that no one believes that I don't understand — they laugh.

Finally, I sat down at the desk, dipped my pen in ink, and wrote: "Classification": then, having thought a bit: "Section,"; then, having thought a bit more: "Subsection." On the right and on the left. Then I froze.

I worked for 5 1/2 months, two more weeks — and vacation (with salary). *But I can't take it.* And the last three months of clippings aren't pasted up. And they're starting to suspect my *yat'* "Come on, comrade, haven't you gotten used to the new spelling yet?". . . The classification has to be presented by the 28th. At the very latest. I have to be fair — communists are trusting and patient. An old regime institution would have taken one look at me and fired me immediately. Here, I myself resign.

The director, M—r, reading my letter of resignation, briefly:

"Better conditions?"

"Military rations and discounted meals for all family members."

(Faster than a flash of lightning, a brazen invention.)

"Then I couldn't possibly keep you. But be careful: those kinds of institutions can fall apart quickly."

"I'm an executive."

"On whose recommendation?"

"Two *pre*-October Party members."

"What's your position?"

"Translator."

"Translators are needed. I wish you success."

I leave. I'm already at the door — and he calls out:

"Comrade Efron, you'll be presenting the classification, of course?"

I, pleading:

"All the materials are there. . . . My assistant will have no problem. . . . Or just deduct it from my salary!"

They didn't deduct it. No, hand on heart, I can say that to this day I, personally, haven't seen communists do anything bad (maybe I haven't seen any bad communists!). And it isn't them I hate, but

31

communism (for two years now all I've heard everywhere is "Communism is wonderful, but communists – are horrid!" I'm sick and tired of it!)

But, to return to the classification. (Illumination: isn't this the entire essence of communism?! – exactly the same as at 15 with algebra, at seven – with arithmetic!). Full eyes and an empty page. The same with cutting patterns – *I don't understand,* I don't understand: what's left, what's right, my temples whirl, there's a lead weight on my brow. It used to be the same with selling at the market – with hiring servants, with all of my hundred-pood earthly life: I *don't* understand, I *can't* stand it, it *doesn't* work out.

I think that if others were forced to write *Fortuna,* they would feel the same.

*   *   *

I go to work at Monplenbezh – in the card file.

April 26th, 1919.

I've only just returned, and I've made a momentous vow: I'm not going to work at a job. Never. Even if I die.

It happened this way. Smolensky Boulevard, a building in the garden. I enter. The room is like a coffin. The walls are made of index cards: not a ray of light. The air is paper (not noble, like book paper, but – ashen. Thus, the difference between a library and a card catalogue file: there you breath the air of refuge, here – of refuse!). Frighteningly elegant ladies (coworkers). In bows and "boots." They look you over – and despise you. I sit opposite a grill-covered window, the Russian alphabet in my hands. The cards have to be separated by letters. Everything with A, everything with B, then by the second letters, i.e.: Abrikosov, Avdeev, then by the third letters. From 9 in the morning until 5:30 in the evening. The lunch is expensive, I won't be eating. Previously, they gave out this and that, now they don't give out anything. I missed the Easter rations. The directress – is a short-legged, forty-year-old ungainly cuttlefish in a corset, in spectacles – terrifying. I smell a former inspectress and a current prison guard. With caustic frankness she's astounded at my slowness: "we average two hundred cards a day. You obviously aren't familiar with this.". . .

I cry. A stony face and tears like cobblestones. It probably looks more like a tin idol melting than a woman weeping. No one sees because no one raises their brow: they're competing for speed.

"I've done this many cards!"

"I've done this many!"

And suddenly, I don't know why, I stand up, collect my belongings, and approach the directress:

"I didn't sign up for lunch today, may I run home?"

A perspicacious, bespectacled look:

"Do you live far?"

"Nearby."

"But be back here in half an hour. This sort of thing isn't done here."

"Oh, of course."

I leave – still a statue. At Smolensky market, tears – a torrent. Some woman, frightened:

"They've robbed you? have they Miss?!"

And suddenly – laughter! Exultation! Sun full on my face! It's over. Nowhere. Never.

It wasn't I who left the card file: my legs carried me. From soul to legs: without going through the mind. This is what instinct is. [. . .]

*Translated by Jamey Gambrell*

© by Jamey Gambrell 1990

# Evgenia Ginzburg

## "DON'T CRY IN FRONT OF THEM"

### Chapter from the book *WITHIN THE WHIRLWIND*

After Colonel Franko's magical order, arrangements for Vasya's journey went through other channels – channels in which the affairs of ex-prisoners were an insignificant part of the traffic. These channels were specially designed for bringing out to Kolyma people who were wanted and needed there. Now things moved much more quickly.

When the Kazan militia courteously handed over to Vasya a first-class set of documents assuring his entry into a secret, banned zone, the Aksyonovs were beside themselves with excitement. But they began to wonder: How could an outlaw who played the piano in a kindergarten procure such splendid documents? They sent me an embarrassed letter in which they congratulated me on my "comeback" but also changed their tune on the subject of Vasya. They were kindly people and in the ten years he had been with them they had become attached to the boy. Although over the past two years he had almost worn them down with his wayward behavior and they themselves had demanded that I take him off their hands, now that it had become a practical possibility they were afraid to send him on such a long joirney.

"Why not let him finish school here?" they wrote.

A new obstacle had arisen unexpectedly. It would be the last straw if my reunion with Vasya were to be wrecked now, after the ordeals I had gone through to get him a travel permit. But my anxiety was superfluous. I had an ally in Vasya himself. For the first time since our parting twelve years before I started to receive letters from him in which I caught glimpses of my unknown son's personality. Instead of the terse little notes he had previously sent ("How are you? We are all right. How is the weather where you are? It's all right here," etc.), I began to get emphatic assertions that he had received the pass and would definitely be coming. Was it

34

true that Kolyma was a stone's throw from Alaska? And was it true that there were tribes in Kolyma related to the Iroquois?

I read and reread these sheets of paper covered with the unformed handwriting of a teenager, and I could vividly picture to myself my little boy tossing about at night on the couch in the Aksyonovs' dining room, dreaming of becoming an explorer like La Pérouse or Vasco da Gama, of sailing through meandering, green inlets between cliffs of basalt and pearl. I realized how ardently he longed for adventure on some distant voyage, he who had as yet seen nothing in his life other than an orphaned childhood in a family of not particilarly close relatives and a dull, regimented school of the forties.

For the first time we were connected by a thin thread of unspoken understanding. Now I knew how to write to him: instead of reminding about our family life of long ago, about which he could remember nothing, I now dwelled on descriptions of Kolyma's exotic scenery, on the dangers of the journey by sea. I asked what means of transport he preferred, sea or air. . . . Anton got him a dagger made from a walrus tusk and decorated by Chukchi ivory carvers, and I gave Vasya a detailed description of the dagger and of the Chukchi way of life (of which I knew at the time only what others had told me). I got in reply every time the same impatient question: "When will it be?"

He was scheduled to arrive at the beginning of September so as not to miss out on the school year. With my heart in my mouth, I paid a visit to what was then the one and only secondary school in Magadan and had a talk with the director of studies; I explained that my son was to arrive shortly and asked whether they had a vacancy in the ninth class. . . . It was a sharp, prickly feeling of re-emerging from the land of nightmares into the land of ordinary, rational human activity. What a wonderful thing it was to be, just for a moment, someone like all the others. Not a prisoner in solitary, not in transit, not an accused before the Military Collegium, not a terrorist-detainee. Just a mother visiting a school to register her son.

But for the time being these were all pipe dreams. There were many hurdles yet before our reunion became a reality. First of all, I had to find the fare. Where was I to get it from? Plane fare would be three thousand rubles. Another question was: Who would accompany him? Although Vasya was nearly sixteen, and the journey out to Magadan had become somewhat easier over the years, expecially for free persons, I was still in thrall to old notions: to my mind, my son was still an infant and the journey was still as hard as it had been when I had made it under escort. I simply could not entertain the thought of my child making such a journey all alone.

Julia undertook to find the money.

"I've already passed the word around among the people we know. We'll get it together. . . . After all, he'll be the first mainland child of an ex-prisoner to come out to Kolyma. What do you mean, charity? What rubbish! It's a loan, of course. I've told them all that we will pay it back in the course of the year."

But then something occured that made the collection unneccessary. It suddenly emerged that one of Julia's helpers in the workshop was a secret millionaire. Well, not a millionaire but a "thousandaire" - Aunt Dusya.

Aunt Dusya was an expert knitter of wool sweaters and had established a clientele among the Kolyma elite. Apart from that, her old mother had recently died, bequething to the sixty-year-old Dusya a stout log cabin with shutters. Some distant relatives had written to ask Dusya whether she would be coming to take possession of her legacy. If not, perhaps she would assign the house to them and they would see she didn't lose by this transaction. After a brief exchange of letters, Dusya had received a money order for five thousand rubles.

Julia was the only person to whom Aunt Dusya had confided all this. She had kept it a secret from the others since she was afraid of arousing their envy. Aunt Dusya kept her savings book in Julia's iron safe, which contained all the documentation of the workshop. In her everyday dealings Aunt Dusya was thrifty almost to the point of miserliness. For example, whenever a big pot of soup was made for everybody in the workshop, Aunt Dusya wouldn't let anybody skim it, because she maintained it was the scum that contained the most nourishing protein.

It was Aunt Dusya who became my principal creditor. She chose to visit us late at night, when all our neighbors were already sleeping, sat down on the bed in her quilted jacket, looked around at the thin walls through which the least sound from the adjoining match boxes could be heard, and put her finger to her lips.

"Shh . . . shh . . . The main thing is to get it all settled nice and quickly, so people can't tittle-tattle," she whispered, rummaging in the recesses of her jacket. "Here, take it! Three, exactly, for the plane ticket. For all the odds and ends, you can borrow from somebody else. Only please dont tell anybody that I've handed out so much money. People'll start to get envious, and I don't like that."

Large hundred-ruble notes, colorful, imposing, brand-new, lay there in a solid wad on the rickety little table. Thirty of them. Radiant, resplendent, incredible. They troubled us.

"It's an awful lot, Aunt Dusya," said Julia. "Perhaps we'd do better to try and get everyone to chip in a bit, so that you're not the only one to carry the burden."

"What's the point of fooling around? Take it, since I've given it to you! It's not as if I'm throwing the money away – it's on loan."

"Of course! I'll pay it back within the year, Dusya. But perhaps you'd feel happier if I gave you a receipt," I ventured.

A look of mild irritation flitted across Aunt Dusya's face.

"You know the saying: 'Don't accept a blow; don't refuse a gift.' What would be the point of giving me a receipt? Birds of passage, that's what we are. Here today, gone tomorrow . . . If your lucky number comes up, you can let me have it sooner. You think I shouldn't take your word for it? We've known each other some time now. . . ."

Aunt Dusya counted the hundred-ruble notes again, patted them into a neat rectangle, and stroked the pile with a broad palm coarsened by tree felling.

"Surprised?" she again muttered indignantly. "You're thinking: Why has the old skinflint suddenly coughed up? Well, that just goes to show you how much you understand about people! Just because I won't give the girls money to go to the movies, you think I'm some sort of miser. What's the point of us going to the movie? A zek's life is a sight more interesting than anything you'd see in any movie. But this is something really important. The first time zek's son is coming from the mainland. If mine were alive and coming here, you wouldn't refuse me a loan, would you? Well, that's how it is. . . I have to go. . . You get to bed now. . . ."

(Aunt Dusya's only son had been killed in the first year of the war. The most shameful thing was that when she was handing over the money neither I nor Julia had managed to remember this. Aunt Dusya never spoke of it. She had been unberably hurt when the notification of his death had been addressed not to her – as if she were not her son's mother – but to some distant aunt. It seemed to her that this humiliation cast a shadow also on her son's memory.)

I now had the money for the ticket. There remained the matter of finding an escort. It was Anton who found a traveling companion. In the free hospital where he was working, one of the serious cardiac cases was a man named Kozyrev, the chief accountant at Dalstroi. His was a long, hopeless illness. By pure chance the free doctor went away, and for a short time Kozyrev was handed over to Anton's care. Anton had him for two weeks, during which time the patient got considerably better. No one could understand what caused the improvement. Perhaps a change in the atmospheric pressure? More likely, the influence of psychotherapy, at which Anton was without equal. (To tease him I used to say that he was more of a priest than a doctor.)

But then the free doctor in charge of the case returned and took from Anton, and . . . the patitnt took a sharp turn for the worse. Kozyrev's wife, Nina Konstantinovna, a cashier in a food store, rushed around trying to persuade the administration to have her husband transferred to the ward for which Walter was responsible. They pointed out that there were only ex-zeks in that ward. They appealed to her political sense and tried to convince her that the transfer of a patient from a free doctor to a prisoner-doctor and a German at that - might have undesirable political overtones. This wrangle was still in progress when the patient died. In all probability, even Anton could not have brought him back to health, at least that was what he thought himself. But no one could change the widow's mind: if her husband had remained in Dr. Walter's care, he would still be alive.

After the funeral the widow collapsed with grief. She decided not to go to the hospital for treatment; she had Anton attend her at home. He paid her daily visits. The sick woman recovered and became passionately devoted to the doctor. She would do anything for him. When he told her the story of our efforts to bring Vasya out, she categorically announced: "It so happens that I'm going on the mainland. I'll bring him back."

She was a lean, nimble woman of fifty, with small, quick eyes. She never made a mistake in counting out the change at her cash desk. Her arithmetic, though, was better than her Russian. She spoke in the accent of the lower-middle-class suburbs of Moscow, and couldn't even get her own patronymic right: "Konstantinovna" became "Kiskinkinovna." But she had a tender heart and, still more important, a will of her own. She made up her own mind about who was good and who was bad, without having to consult their personal file. She didn't give a damn about Anton's articles, about his period of imprisonment, or even about his being a German. She knew just one thing: he had saved her, and he would indubitably have saved her husband if they had let him, the skunks! . . .

In the matter of bringing Vasya out to Kolyma she showed

herself to be not only kindhearted but also determined. Her daughter Tamara married to an MGB interrogator who strongly objected to his mother-in-law's getting mixed up with the son of someone who had a political record. But Nina Konstantinovna simply ignored these domestic complications and went her own way.

At this stage, when things seemed to be turning out so favorably, I became more nervous than ever. I was haunted night and day by the fear that some fatal mishap might prevent Vasya's arrival. Suppose he fell ill. . . Suppose the Aksyonovs dug their heels in. . . . Suppose he changed his mind. . . . Suppose Kozyreva changed her mind. . . . But no, she stuck to her guns. In May she invited me to her apartment, choosing an hour when her son-in-law would be away at work. I went along at the appointed hour and handed over Dusya's three thousand rubles for Vasya's airfare.

"Right, then," she said, rapidly counting the notes and screwing up her small, inquisitive eyes at me. "Right! You can stop worrying. I said I'd bring him and I will. For the doctor's sake . . . How many years has it been since you've seen your boy? Twelve years? How on earth did you hold on? No one would guess to look at you that you had grieved for him so much. You look in pretty good shape."

In June I raised another thousand in small loans and sent it off to Mother in Rybinsk to enable her to go to Kazan, get Vasya fitted out, and take him to Moscow, where Kozyreva would be awaiting him. This was a year and a half before Mother's death. But she concealed from me how ill she was feeling, how difficult the journey was for her. It was only afterward that I recalled the part in her letter where she had written: "How I used to love the trips on the Volga! But lately I haven't been feeling too well, even when I travel by boat. But none of that matters. The important thing is for you and little Vasya to be together again."

In July I received news that Vasya was already in Moscow, in the Kozyrevs' apartment on Sretenka Street. Mother had handed him over personally to Nina Konstantinovna, and had gone home to Rybinsk. Vasya was enchanted with Moscow, with his own freedom, with his friendship with the unruly son of the Kozyrev family, Volodya, who had dropped out of school. He was now a taxi driver, and was driving Vasya around Moscow to show him the sights. Vasya and Nina Konstantinovna would soon be taking the plane to Magadan.

But July and August passed, and all my phone calls to the MGB interrogator's apartment elicited one and the same answer: Nina Konstantinovna had been delayed for family reasons. In September I was due to leave town and go with the kindergarten to the health camp again. I felt quite desperate. He would arrive in my absence. . . . But October came around. School had begun a month before. I was back from the Northern Artek Pioneer camp, and still there was no sign of Nina Kozyreva and Vasya.

My nervous tension mounted. Vasya was so skimpily dressed that he would freeze, having to fly in late autumn. He might have to miss a year of school. . . . But all these reasonable daytime fears were nothing compared with my dark, nighttime forebodings, which were utterly irrational. Perhaps as a result of someone's evil designs I was doomed to lose both my children. Alyosha was no more. . . . And Vasya, the last spark of my now almost extinct life would either board the plane and perish somewhere up in the clouds or else simply disappear into thin air. And again, as during those sleepless nights at Elgen, I heard the formula of despair hammering in my ears: "No one will ever call me Mother again."

Both Anton and Julia daily expended a vast quantity of words, angry words and loving words, to bring me to my senses.

"It'll end up with his arriving and your not being here to greet him," Julia predicted gloomily. "You don't eat, drink, or sleep. . . . How much longer can it go on?"

"You're ungrateful," Anton said with fury. "You're the only ex-zek who's managed to get permission for her son to come out here, and all you do is . . ."

"Please don't say that. You'll bring me bad luck."

At this Anton mounted his hobbyhorse. He proclaimed that he had met no more superstitious people in the prisons and camps than the former Communists. They believed in literally anything, in any sort of sign or manifestation. . . . If only I believed in God as much as I did in all those idiocies. . . .

Here Julia broke in, and they both ignored me and started to argue among themselves. Julia, who almost from the cradle had had it drummed firmly into her head that religion was the opium of the people, could not bear hearing Anton hold forth on the difference between faith and superstition.

"It's quite extraordinary, Anton Yakovlevich, how you, a person with excellent training in biology, can repeat such fables."

"What is much stranger, Julia Pavlovna, is to find you, a person educated in philosophy, repeating the flattest of platitudes and refusing to draw conclusions from the lessons that we all learned in prison."

I left them to pursue their interminable argument and strolled off to the watchman's room in Julia's workshop next door, to phone the Kozyrev's.

"Tell me, please, has Nina Konstantinovna arrived?"

"No, not yet."

The receiver was slammed down directly in my ear, to cut short my questions. There followed a long succession of wearisome days, each of which began in hope and ended in despair.

Meanwhile Julia and I had moved into the new apartment. She had been given an official order entitling her to an entire fifteen square meters in view of the enlargement of the family: namely, Vasya's imminent arrival. Our new building was next door to the old one, but it was two stories high, and our apartment was on the second floor. There were at least twenty rooms along the corridor. Ours was one of the best – or perhaps that was only how it seemed to us at the time. In any event, it really did measure fifteen square meters, and it had a good window. Julia had somehow obtained a screen, and we used it to partition off a separate corner for Vasya. He had an iron bed, a chair, and a small table; on the table were an inkpot, paper, and textbooks for the ninth class. We had laid in for Vasya a woolen blanket and a real feather pillow, which Julia bore in as if it were a trophy, holding it above her head, her eyes flashing triumphantly. Anton had tucked under the pillow a set of new underwear, socks, and two shirts. He had obtained all this in exchange for a large number of his bread rations at the quarantine center.

And so Kolyma prepared to greet my schoolboy son with a first-rate set of standard camp clothing.

Far from thanking my faithful friends, I scolded them, seeking an outlet for my frustrated longing and my anxiety. At times I showered unjust accusations on them.

"Of course . . . it's easy for you to wait calmly. . . . It isn't your only remaining child who's missing."

They didn't take offense. They understood, and they put up with me.

But one day . . . I took the receiver off the hook and with a feeling of numb hopelessness began inquiring whether Nina Konstantinovna had arrived, making my voice sound as impersonal as that of the announcer of the correct time. Suddenly, instead of a blunt, peremptory no, I heard the cheerful, even overcheerful, voice of a tipsy man.

"Yes, she's arrived. We're celebrating. And drinking to her health."

"Oh . . . tell me, what about the boy? Was the boy from Kazan on the plane with her?"

"The boy?"

At that point in the conversation someone came up to whoever I was talking to and asked him something. His attention was diverted, and he began giving someone instructions about plates and dishes, in the same jolly voice. . . . He made a joke of it, and the other person laughed loudly in reply.

How long did that pause in our conversation last? A minute? An eternity? In any case, I had time enough to visualize with appalling clarity all the possible variants of Vasya's tragic end. All the cars in Moscow had combined to run him over. The entire criminal population of Vladivostok or Khabarovsk had robbed him and left him for dead. All the MGB personnel in all those towns had pulled him in for some careless word he had let drop. Any moment now and the same cheerful voice would be saying no, the boy had not arrived. . . .

"The boy? You mean the boy from Kazan? Yes, he's sitting here on the couch. He's worried that they're taking so long to come for him. . . . He's refused champagne, the little teetotaler. . . ."

Another burst of laughter. Then someone took the receiver from my merry interlocutor and said in a hard, hostile voice:

"Why don't you come and pick up your son, madam? He knows your address, but you can't expect him to find his way around in a strange place all at once. And there's nobody here to go with him. Anybody would think we'd done enough getting him here from the mainland."

"I'm on my way . . . this very moment. . . . I didn't know."

I put the receiver down. I wanted to run. But something strange had happened to me. My legs were glued to the floor; they felt weightless, as if made of cotton wool. As though from a great distance, I heard the voice of the watchman on duty:

"Dear me, dear me . . . What's the matter, lady? Looks like you're on your last legs!"

He struck his head out of the inspection window and shouted across to someone:

"Run to Karepova! Tell her her relative's keeling over."

Julia arrived on the scene. Valerian drops and validol were administered.

"Pull yourself together. I'll go with you." Julia, too, was excited and flustered.

The scene that greeted our eyes in the Kozyrevs' flat was reminiscent of a shot from one of those early films showing White Guard officers having a debauch. We cooled our heels in the entrance hall, waiting for Nina Konstantinovna to come out, and through the half-open door we could see the glint of epaulettes and the flushed faces, and we heard the tinkling of glasses, bursts of laughter, and drunken shouts.

"Oh, it's you, is it? He's been waiting so long he's getting really miserable." She hospitably invited us in. "There are two of you, are there? I wonder whether he'll know which is his mother."

She was so eager to embellish what was bound to be an interesting and touching spectacle – a recognition scene, as she thought.

"Watch, Tamara," she called to her daughter, the interrogator's wife. "It'll be just like at the movies," and turning toward the couch, she went on:

"Look, Vasya, my pet. Do you see? Two ladies . . . One of them has to be your mother. You must choose: Which one?"

It was only then that my eyes found the person I had been vainly trying to pick out in the drunken hurly-burly. There he was! A thin teenager in a frayed jacket sitting awkwardly huddled up in one corner of a vast couch.

He rose to his feet. He seemed quite tall and broad in the shoulders. He bore no resemblance whatsoever to the tow-haired, four-year-old roly-poly who used to toddle around our large apartment in Kazan twelve years back. That child, with his fair hair and his blue eyes, had resembled the country children of the Ryazan branch of the Aksyonov family. But this one, the sixteen-year-old, had chestnut hair, and gray eyes that at a distance looked hazel like Alyosha's. Altogether, he was like Alyosha rather than his earlier self.

All these observations were registered by someone who existed quite independently of me. I myself, benumbed and incapable of articulate thought, had to direct all my efforts toward remaining upright and not crumpling up in a heap from the dull thudding of the blood rushing to my temples, my neck, my face. . . .

He did not hesitate between Julia and myself. He came up to me and self-consciously put his hand on my shoulder. And then I heard at long last the word that I had been afraid of never hearing again, that now came to me across a gulf of almost twelve years, from the time before all those courts, prisons, and penal drafts, before the death of my first-born, before all those nights in Elgen.

"Mother," said my son, Vasya.

"He recognized you," Kozyreva exclaimed in delight. "That's blood speaking. It always does. . . . You see, Tamara?"

His eyes were definitely not hazel. Not like Alyosha's. Alyosha's hazel eyes were closed forever. They could not come back again. And yet . . . How much he resembled Alyosha as he was then, at the age of ten – no, nearly eleven. My two sons had for an instant merged into one and the same image.

"Alyosha, my darling," I said in a whisper, almost involuntarily. Suddenly I heard a deep, muffled voice: "No, Mamma. I'm not Alyosha. I'm Vasya."

And then in a rapid whisper into my ear:

"Don't cry in front of them. . . . "

Thereupon I took hold of myself. I looked at him in the way that those who are really close, who know everything about one another. He understood my look. It was the most crucial moment in my life: the joining up of the broken links in our chain of time; the recapturing of our organic closeness severed by twelve years of separation, of living among strangers. My son! And he knew, even though I hadn't said a word to him, who we were and who they were. He appealed to me not to demean myself in their presence.

"Don't be afraid, my dear. . . . I won't cry," my look said to him. And aloud, in a matter-of-fact, almost calm voice:

"Say thank you to Nina Konstantinovna, Vasya, and let's go home. It's time."

*Translated by Ian Boland*

# I. Grekova

## UNDER THE STREET LAMP

It was cold outside — a rushing, coal-black autumn evening. A sharp wind blew from one direction, then from another, tossing about clumps of fallen leaves and raindrops. The street lamp swung back and forth on its cable like a lunatic. Behind the street lamp, a black shadow swung along the sidewalk just as frantically. Because of the wind, everything outside seemed to be astir, everything seemed to be displaced, moving, even the walls of houses seemed to tilt.

Two people stood on the corner — a man and a woman. He was tall, bare-headed, with sharp muscles on his thin, weather-beaten face. The wind whipped and tossed his straight blond hair. In the bouncing light of the street lamp, mobile, angular shadows kept appearing and disappearing on his face.

The woman was not terribly remarkable, a brunette with a white silk scarf on her disheveled hair. The scarf fluttered in the wind and swelled, wisps of her hair flew about and were tossed from side to side. Transparent raindrops flickered and died out on her face.

He held her hand and looked down into her face, and she answered by looking up into his. In the shifting shadows his eyes were almost terrifying in their expressiveness, as if they could not stand up to the pressure from within; they gave in, stirred, drifted off, went out of focus. Looking into these eyes, she felt a vague pain inside her, like the one you feel in an elevator when it starts its descent right after you press the button.

She said something. The wind whipped away the beginning of her sentence, so that he heard only the end:

". . . just think, a difference of eight years."

"I couldn't care less about that," he said harshly and looked down at the ground. His face and eyes immediately turned harsh, came back into focus. He tapped his foot on a disintegrating yellow maple leaf and repeated:

"I couldn't care less about that."

"Tomorrow. Tomorrow I'll tell you everything. But now I have to go. Please . . . until tomorrow."

She grabbed the door handle. He leaned over and kissed her, not on the mouth and not on the cheek, but somewhere by her lips. Her lips were both cold and warm, covered in raindrops. She went inside.

\* \* \*

Tatiana Vasilievna walked up the stairs, opened the common door with one key and then her own door with another.

She had two rooms in the sleepy communal — former lordly — apartment, two almost separate rooms: a small apartment within a large one. The rooms had at one time been made from one, the former living room: they divided it with a partition, and each room got a window and half a splendid stucco rosette, from the middle of which had once hung a chandelier. It turned out fine, it was even possible to carve out a small foyer. It's just that the tall ceilings were totally out of proportion with the rooms. When they were little, the boys use to say, "Our rooms are taller than they are long."

In the foyer, she took off and shook out her raincoat and scarf. It was quiet. There was no one in the small apartment. And at this late hour even everyone in the big apartment was asleep: no one was washing in the bathroom or pattering along the corridor. Only the electric meter over the door purred, counting out its time in energy.

She hesitated a bit, stood in the foyer, touched that spot by her lips where she had just been kissed. The kiss was strange somehow, not on the mouth and not on the cheek, but both places at once. She remembered and once again had that elevator feeling which was hard to identify as either pleasant or painful. No, not now. You have to think. Tomorrow you have to tell him something.

The apartment was empty and quiet, there was no one to keep her from thinking. The children were all off somewhere: Katya was doing an internship, Tolya and Volya were potato harvesting. She turned on the table lamp, sat down, and picked up a pencil: it was her habit to think with something in her hand.

46

So. This crazy day was over — the wind, flying leaves, the bouncing street lamp. How everything rushed headlong when they were on their endless walk: along the streets and boulevards smelling of the earth, smelling of fallen leaves; along the embankments, where lights were stuck in the water like long gold nails. They walked, wound up in front of her house, and she went in. She went in to think.

She was at home. These two rooms — a small apartment in a big one — were her home. A lot of years, what can you say, a lot of years. Here, in these two rooms, her children had grown up, became adults. The rooms were neither very cozy, nor very clean. Almost all her friends — "other people" — had cozier, cleaner homes. As they say in novels: "One could sense a caring, feminine hand everywhere." Here one didn't sense it. What kind of a mistress of the house was she? For a long time now she's been the head of the household. Head of the household and mistress of the house in one person. Can one person be two real people? In books, yes, in life, no.

Tatiana Vasilievna worked like a man and fought with everyday life like a woman. It was hard to say which was more difficult — probably everyday life, after all. She loved her scientific work without reflection, without declarations — she just loved it. Like a worn-out pair of slippers. Those marvelous moments of success — when a conjecture about "why it was so" would suddenly and miraculously illuminate the dark muddle of facts — were not all that frequent. Much more often she experienced patient scientific workdays with no sparks, just diligence. While inside, slowly, like water under the ice, thought murmered and labored. Time was at a premium: lectures, articles, conferences, labs. The laboratory was the most important of all — her baby. That's how she lived. They say she'd gotten somewhere. Along the way, the children had somehow grown up into good children. . . . But no, she didn't keep the apartment spiffed up. She did only what had to get done so that the dirt wouldn't take over. Still, she always wanted it to be like other people's homes, longed for noble appearances. Sometimes on a Sunday, Tatiana Vasilievna — in a lab coat, with a bucket and rag in her hand, and feeling like a worrier — would start cleaning. On days like this the children would say: "A Sunday mother is a nightmare; the sooner Monday comes the better." She herself preferred Mondays. The worst thing was that it was all for nothing. Cleaning took a great deal of effort, while its effects disappeared all too quickly. Within two or three days, hordes of books would appear, and articles of clothing, and radios – and make themselves at home in the apartment. The furniture had once been good but was now old and falling into decay. Tolya called the furniture "the sparkle and poverty of courtesans." This year, especially, it had somehow suddenly started to fall apart. Volya did his drawing on the dinner table – an old mahogany one – and suddenly it fell apart under his elbows. Volya cursed, and Tolya, as always, made ironical comments, then both of them, shoving and quarreling, put the legs of the table together using an ordinary board. There was talk of "calling a carpenter," but things never got past the stage of talk. The table stood to this day with a pine board connecting mahogany legs. The other furniture, though – a sofa and two chairs – was reupholstered last year. Tatiana Vasilievna was very proud: she had reupholstered the furniture, her home was like other people's. . . . An old reupholsterer had been recommended and called in. For two weeks he was king of the apartment: he made a mess, smoked, sang songs; in the third week he started drinking and disappeared. Tatiana Vasilievna went to his house, begged, cajoled, brought him back almost by force, and he fell asleep on the sofa, which was turned inside out. Yes, they went through a lot before the sofa and chairs took their places in their fancy new clothes. They stood there pretty and obedient, like well-brought-up children, and every time she came home from work, Tatiana Vasilievna took pleasure in looking at them. She even started thinking about new housekeeping feats, such as liquidating all the junk. An incredible amount of junk had accumulated. Books were the worst. They seemed to multiply all on their on. They were everywere: big ones and little ones, hard cover and paper back, old and new. In fact, the real residents of the apartment were books; people were incidental. Like Chekhov's sisters dreaming about an unattainable Moscow, Tatiana Vasilievna dreamed about sorting out the books and calling a second-hand bookseller. She would sometimes even commence the task and drag the children into it. Nothing would come of it. It always ended with some bizarre, long-forgotten books coming out of hiding which it was simply impossible not to take a look at. Well, and then, instead of a book sorting, it would turn into what they called a "reading room." The whole family would sit among scattered piles of books, reading ecstatically.

After books, old shoes took second place in the apartment. Various and sundry pumps, loafers, work shoes, overshoes, boots, snow boots. They jostled in the foyer and grazed under the beds like dusty strays. Nobody really wore them, but it was a pity and a shame to throw them away. . . . Since childhood, Tatiana Vasilievna believed that you could sell old stuff "to Tartars." But "Tartars" somehow never came — apparently people of this nationality now did other things. It would be nice to give the shoes to someone, preferably wholesale, but to whom? No, it was embarrassing to offer anyone such a gift. Wouldn't I be offended of someone gave me old pumps? Yes, I would. Once she stealthily took out an old pair of shoes and put them on the landing: maybe somebody would take them. Fat chance! The next day the shoes were brazenly standing just as before, even sort of defiantly, and she diffidently brought them back in.

When they had reupholstered the furniture, it suddenly seemed to her that anything was possible. Just wait, I'll manage both the books and the shoes. But then Volya spilled a bottle of India ink in the fancy new chair, and Tatiana Vasilievna, to her own dismay, was almost unmoved, even a little glad: now she could once again forget about the second-hand bookseller. . . .

Oh, the children. They were constantly spoiling something or getting it dirty. Good children, golden children, but — why hide it! — they were somehow disorderly. Even Katya. Dear, thin little Katya. An ear of grain on a long blade of straw.

The most characteristic thing about Katya was her intense conscience. It was as if she didn't live but just asked herself and others: Am I living correctly? Am I doing it right? And that's the way it was from her early childhood. A funny little girl with thin, pale little pigtailes, with unsmiling, reproachful eyes of a stern gray, she stood before her elders like a living question — a question and a demand. A reproach. But she was herself unskillful, untidy; she couldn't do anything right. She couldn't even darn her socks. She never managed to learn how. But to teach her one needed time, oh! so much time, so much more than to do it oneself. Tatiana Vasilievna wasn't home much, and in her absence Katya read and read, like one possessed. To tear her away from a book was as difficult as rousing a drunk. It was difficult and a shame when she raised her eyes and, with an expression of tense suffering, tried to understand what on earth they wanted from her.

Katya had stretched out, but still remained the same. Slender, but not graceful, awkward, rather. With childish, flat-heeled shoes on her feet. No guile: her thin, pale hair was combed very flat, pulled back from her blue temples. And her eyes still asked everyone: Are you living right? Are you living correctly? She had decided for herself to go to medical school, become a surgeon, and now she was suffering, doubting herself. . . . Sometimes she would come home lifeless and stare into space, and it seemed you could hear her thinking: I'm untalented.

She never had any boyfriends, but last year one had turned up, hung around for a while, and then didn't come back. A good-looking boy, straightforward, fun loving. They could have gone out together, simply and for fun. But it didn't work — that's Katya for you. Every step is a tragedy with her. She doesn't know how to dance, or, rather, she's embarrassed to. When the kids get together and sing, she just silently looks on with her huge eyes, and the others start feeling uncomfortable, as if they're doing something wrong. They ask her why she doesn't sing. She answers that she doesn't have a good voice. It's not true. Tatiana Vasilievna heard her singing once while she was washing the floor and thought no one was home. Her voice was thin and shy, but clear as a bell.

. . . My poor Katya. It's hard for you. I know myself. Two giftless people. . . .

The boys — Tolya and Volya — now they're different. Tatiana Vasilievna involuntarily smiled as she thought of those two — together, as always. The twins grew up together, sat next to each other at school, now at college. . . . And they constantly fought and argued. When they were small, the fighting never stopped, as if there was a motor running in the house all the time. When Tatiana Vasilievna would get home, the first thing she would do was listen: Is everything okay? How's the motor, is it running? If everything was quiet, she knew something was wrong: either one of the boys was sick, or they were both plotting some kind of outrageous mischief. They both had a knack for technical things from an early age, and all their mischief had an industrial bent, such as taking apart the wall clock to supplement their building set or making a gear for the meat grinder out of a woman's bicycle. . . . Outwardly they didn't look at all alike — it was hard to believe they were twins. Volya was dark and stocky, with twinkling black eyes, one of which was a little crossed.

Tolya was pale, with ash-blond hair and a pensive smile which put a deep dimple in his left cheek. Their father would say that Tolya and Volya must have started fighting while they were still in their mother's womb and that's why they came out that way: one a little cross-eyed, the other with one dimple.

Time passed, the brothers grew and grew up, but they still fought. It's funny that they are grown young men who shave, and yet not long ago they fought over some book. Even now they must be fighting out there at the state farm harvesting potatoes, the motor is running, everything's okay. They fight, but they can't live without each other. Volya's an enthusiast, an inventor, a bragger who picks fights; he's messy, constantly losing things. Tolya is a skeptic, a scoffer, modest, smart, a merciless critic of Volya's nonsensical ideas. He keeps his things neat and in order (Volya doesn't recognize the division into "mine" and "yours"). Volya's a good-looking young man with bushy eyebrows and a burning gaze. His crossed eye was barely noticeable now, it even suited him — made his gaze even more burning and wild. Tolya's invisible next to him — narrow in the shoulders, stooped over. His only charm is his smile — that rare, priceless dimpled smile. When you see it, it seems that there's no person on earth more handsome and sweet. My dear boys. Brother-brigands.

Think. You have to think. You told him yourself that tomorrow you'd tell him everything.

Tatiana Vasilievna walked up to the mirror to comb her hair out for the night, take the pins out of her thin, tangled hair. She ran a comb through one strand and shuddered: out of the half-light of the mirror a still rather young woman was looking at her, familiar, but not entirely. Oh, to freeze in this position, not to move, to look and not believe that this conventional sign of a woman, this phantom was really me. . . . No, it turns out not to be possible to freeze for long. One turn of the head and the phantom is gone.

Tatiana Vasilievna looked good for her age and was used to hearing this from everyone but attached no importance to it. So you look better, you look worse; in the end everyone looks all right. . . . She was never a professional female. Just as some people don't master French or English, she hadn't mastered being female. At one time, when Sasha was still around, many people thought her pretty and told her so. . . . Perhaps it was true. What can you do? In her youth she didn't work on her beauty, now she didn't work on her age. She noticed some gray hair in the mirror, but she'd never start dying her hair. The most unpleasant thing was not when you had to see yourself in the mirror, but at the movies. It turns out that it's not your gray hair or your wrinkles, but your bearing. After that instance, she avoided looking in a mirror for a long time. And now, too, she turned away from it, said out loud, "It's late already," and started to make up her bed. To lie down and think. She wound the alarm clock, turned out the light, and went to bed.

It was perfectly silent for the first seconds. Then gradually the swaying shadows of branches and gliding light patches became visible on the wall. It was from that street lamp. Poor thing, it was still dangling there alone on its cable, and the wind whistled and threw drops around − they were beating against the pane and running down it like tears.

. . . To think, but about what? About herself, about her life. Life was so vast. But today for some reson she had to remember, not her whole life chronologically, but some one episode, one event. She had the feeling that she'd forgotten something important, and that something was in her past. All evening, when she wasn't alone, a certain persistent image kept bothering her, nagging at her and then hiding. She had to capture it, and to do so she started to go through her whole life in her mind, layer by layer, asking herself: Is this where it is? Is this it or not? No, that's not it. And once again: That's not it. Then suddenly, there was a moment when it began to seem that it was a bit "it." Just as in that game, when a person in a blindfold looks for a hidden object, and he's prompted: "cold, cold, warmer, still warmer, hot." That's how it was now, every time her thoughts would come up to a certain layer, a voice would prompt her: "warmer, this is where to look." And so she started to look where it was warmer.

At that time they were living in the Urals, where Tatiana Vasilievna and her institute had been evacuated. Her husband, Sasha − a sinologist, an orientalist − had been called up at the very beginning of the war. She received only one letter from him − a cheerful one with a humorous description of the front−line life of the "boxer−shorts company," as he called his combined, purely civilian unit. There were no more letters, Tatiana Vasilievna wrote but did not get a single answer. She dealt with all possible levels of command but got nowhere. He just disappeared. She got stock, lifeless responses: "addressee unknown," or "address unknown." She was afraid to leave: What if a letter came and she wasn't there? But it was unthinkable not to leave with the institute and so she left, and the children with her – the eldest, Katya, and the boys – and Aunt Marie.

Aunt Marie was Sasha's aunt and had lived with him for a long time, before he was married. Her sister, Sasha's mother, a pretty and vivacious woman, had died long before, but Aunt Marie was alive and by now she was at least seventy-five or so. She was a strange creature, this Aunt Marie. Starting with her exterior: she was exceptionally, pathetically homely. Her right, frightening eye was completely crossed and seemed not to go with her face; it seemed to live on its own, it threatened, it complained. . . . And the face itself – long and red with a blue tinge – seemed to drip down from her forehead. Over this forehead every morning Aunt Marie would erect an elaborate hairdo out of her yellowish-gray hair in the kind of roll that was fashionable at the turn of the century. She was tormented by rheumatism from an early age. Her huge, swollen hands – also red with a blue tinge – stirred in a manner that was somehow disorderly. When Aunt Marie had to take some bread from the table, let's say, or some scissors, her huge hand would sway for a long time, as if it were aiming, before it took the object; it was like a terrible parody of the first grasping movements of an infant. And her feet were the same – huge, swollen, and shuffling. It seemed as if Aunt Marie didn't walk or move but just loitered, and always in those places, in those passageways, through which everyone else – the quick, orderly ones – had to pass. When the necessity arose to do something next to her – pick something up or pass it to someone – Aunt Marie would start convulsively and conscientiously shuffling her feet, but without getting up from her chair.

Tatiana Vasilievna didn't like Aunt Marie very much. She was irritated by the loitering and shuffling. Besides, she thought she could see disapproval in Aunt Marie's enigmatic crossed eye. And rightly so. Aunt Marie disapproved of Tatiana Vasilievna. No, Sasha's wife was not living the way one should with such a husband. A wonderful husband, three children, and she for some reason goes to work, meets with men there. "Coquetting," Aunt Marie thought with reproach but never said this out loud. And whom was she to say it to anyway? She lived by herself somehow, in a corner behind the dresser – which she referred to

53

by the old-fashioned term commode. The commode was a world in itself. Aunt Marie's own personal world. Memories. Ostrich feathers. Ancient lace, fans, gloves. Faded photographs in velvet frames. All this was tied together with ribbons, interlaid with fragrant sachets and emanated some unusual, bookish kind of perfume: lavender. . . .

Little Katya was the only one of the whole family who truly associated with Aunt Marie. She would bring her little stool into Aunt Marie's corner, sit at her swollen feet, touchingly and demandingly raising her adult eyes, and listen to Aunt Marie's stories about the old days. And Aunt Marie, with her shaking head, uncertainly caressing the thin, blond pigtails with her swollen hand, would tell Katya about her youth. How she danced with a shawl at the graduation ball at the young ladies' institute and how she was noticed and praised by the Grand Duke himself (I was dancing with my profile to him, and I was quite pretty from the left side), and finally, lowering her voice, speaking as if only to herself, she would tell about how all her life she loved, madly loved, but one man — "your grandfather, Katya" — and how she gave him up without a fight to her sister, a pretty giggler. And he never found out that she loved him, loves him to this day, although grandfather has been dead for twenty years. And Katya listened and loved grandfather together with Aunt Marie. Sometimes Aunt Marie would take her treasures out of the commode, and among them the portrait of grandfather in a cuirass and fur shako ("was he a tsar or something?"), sorted them, rearranged them, and told the story of each object. She would take out the yellowed lace — "real Alançon" — and say, "I will give this to you when you come out." Katya didn't know what "come out" meant, but she felt that something extraordinary was awaiting her in life, some kind of turning point after which everything would be just as significant and beautiful as in Aunt Marie's life. And she, Katya, would also meet a man and fall in love with him and give him up to another without a fight, and he would never find out that she loved him.

The war came, then the evacuation. Aunt Marie's commode stayed in the abandoned apartment with the boarded-up windows. She took only one little packet with her: grandfather's portrait, several letters, a notebook with a dried rosebud. They were given one room in a dormitory, and in this room Aunt Marie got only a narrow bed in the corner and a small leather

54

traveling-bag under the bed. She didn't understand what was going on, why life had so suddenly changed, why there was no candy and fruit in the house. She knew, after all — that's how up-to-date she was — that children needed fruit, which contained vitamins. And for some reason they weren't buying fruit for the children. And one couldn't walk from room to room — there was only one room. And Aunt Marie grew completely quiet, she even stopped shuffling and spent more and more time sitting or lying on her clumsy metal bed. She silently ate what was given her, sometimes thinking, "It doesn't taste good," but never saying so.

Tatiana Vasilievna, on the other hand, lived on the run, panting, driven by necessity. She lectured at the institute, ran to the market to trade some old clothes for potatoes, dragged bags around, sawed wood, cooked, washed, darned. The household fell apart in her untrained hands and aquired some kind of hostile independence: the primus-stove wouldn't light, the soup burned. And there wasn't enough food. The boys needed milk, and this was acquired in trade for bread. Tatiana Vasilievna almost stopped eating, her cheeks sank, her lips dried up, and a sort of wolf-like gleam appeared in her eyes. When she went to work in the morning, she reeled as if buffeted by the wind, and her feet were so very light, they seemed to belong to someone else. She remembered once going out into the freezing early morning: the sky was a terrifying pink, with clouds of something like smoke or fog, and she walked on her light feet that were someone else's as if she were flying. This morning left a memory of the pink sky and the paradoxical, flying sensation of happiness, communion with the pink sky and the clouds of smoke. But this sensation occurred rarely, maybe only about twice, while usually there was alarm and a consciousness of guilt and responsibility for her little ones, who were so small and dependent. The kids were growing, they had to be fed, although there was little food. Tolya and Volya, looking like potato shoots in a cellar, grew quiet; they even fought lethargically and unwillingly. What was most eerie was their unexpected resemblance. Yes, the poor little things became identical. The same muteness and seriousness appeared in Volya's squinting eye and in Tolya'a dimple, next to which a wrinkle appeared. But what could she do for them? What could she sell, what could she barter? She would stay awake night after night, going through her meager belongings in her mind and calculating: for this they'll give me a dozen eggs,

55

for this a piece of butter, like the one she had recently seen at the market, wrapped in a cabbage leaf. All night in her imagination groceries would line up, trade places, appear in various combinations. Not for herself. She herself didn't need anything. Sugar and butter, which were given out in small quantities for ration cards, had long since become inedible to her, like stones. They were for the children. And Katya, white little Katya, conscience itself, would look at her mother and, swallowing her own saliva, would say, "I don't want it. It's for the boys." Tatiana Vasilievna indeed didn't need anything, once in a while only a small piece of bread and she would certainly have gone to sleep. But no, she couldn't. She would rock herself to sleep, repeating a French saying, picked up lord knows where, "qui dort dine" (he who sleeps, eats). And in fact, if she managed to fall asleep, she would get up in the mouning almost not hungry.

And suddenly, things got unexpectedly easier. It was like a miracle. She, a "high-paid" person, managed to get the boys into a kindergarten. Now, every morning, grown-up, responsible Katya would take the boys "to work," as she called it, one little boy on each side. They argued and from time to time set up a scuffle by way of Katya. They started to fight again: they were being well fed in the kindergarten. Once, Volya even brought Katya a cookie with a raisin. He had picked out the other raisin and eaten it — he couldn't resist.

It got easier, but it was still hard, oh, so hard; the main thing was that she had so little strength, and no water. The water-pipe barely worked. Sometimes the rumor would spread from floor to floor that they were giving out water in the basement across the street. The women, wrapped in shawls, buckets clanging, would run to get water as if there was a fire. Often there wasn't enough for everyone and only the lucky ones who got there first came back with full buckets. Once the yard woman, Dusya, gave a half-bucket of water to Tatiana Vasilievna, who burst into tears out of sheer gratitude and embarrassment. Dusya, also embarrassed, mumbled, "Take it, take it, it's nothing, you're hard up after all." Tatiana Vasilievna understood this perfectly and agreed: she was hard up. She, with her scholarly degree and weak hands was indeed more hard up than all the hard ups in this harsh life. And how many times after this she took charity from strangers for her indigence. Once a colleague at work brought her a whole hundred grams of butter. . . . Another time they collectively gave her a chicken. She didn't refuse; she accepted the charity with seriousness and simplicity, but it was ingraved in her mind. Many years later, when looking at a person, she would say to herself, "That's the one who gave me half a roll once. I remember, I remember well. I will never forget how glad the boys were."

With all of this, life may have been hard, but it was possible if not for the anxiety. The anxiety over the unknown, the terrible apprehension over Sasha. Anxiety resonated through her like a single, undying note. How many letters, sent and returned, and then not even sent. In these letters she would let herself go. She would be tender, superstitious, cowardly – she would be a woman. She would often have this same dream: she, small and weak like a fly, was beating against a big, smooth, impenetrable wall, beating against it and buzzing. She would wake up as if she were having a heart attack and think: maybe at that moment he was in fact killed.

How many widows there were around, how many losses! Was she better or worse off than they? Who knows. . . . They had one burial, while she had thousands of small ones. Every day she buried Sasha and resurrected him again. Her neighbor Nyura got a "burial notice" and Tatiana Vasilievna went to see her. Nyura was sitting on the bed, persistently and efficiently knocking her head against the metal and wailing in a thick, unnatural voice. Next to her stood a runny-nosed little slip of a girl with a drooping stocking who was wailing in unison two octaves higher. Tatiana Vasilievna looked at this scene with a hard heart and no pity. She tried to give Nyura some water, but Nyura kept shaking her head and the water ran down her cheek – that priceless water. How frightened she became then of her hard heart, her thoughts about the water, and one more thought: "Perhaps it is better this way: wail yourself out and get it over with." A terrible thought – no, she couldn't think that way! Her fate was different. And she patiently continued her invisible job of burying and resurrecting. Sometimes her hope was raised high, but it was always followed by despair. These waves always came strictly in pairs. The higher the wave of hope, the higher the wave of despair. The highest pair of waves was right after the end of the war. Many returned, but Sasha did not. Nothing happened; the waves died down. They sometimes returned later on, always in pairs, but each pair was shorter and lower, until finally they disappeared altogether. This was probably about five years after the war. The pain died. In questionnaires under the heading "Family status," Tatiana Vasilievna had long since been writing "widow," but she truly became a widow only when the pain died.

But then, during the war, when everything was still possible, how alive this pain was! The pain was alive, and she herself was alive. Life went on, demanding and full, with difficulties and joys. The lectures were a partcular joy. Arriving at the institute on someone else's light feet, half drunk with weakness and determination, she would walk into the classroom. She'd be met by the distinct, expectant silence of the students. She would begin, and . . . oh! . . . how everything would fall into place. The classroom was like one collective, many-eyed, manageable being. To lead all of them and at the same time to keep track of each pair of eyes.

Before the war in their "difficult" technical college, the girls were as rare as flowers in the grass. Now there was little grass, almost all flowers. And how touching these flowers were − pale, poorly dressed, half starving, yet still not lacking the eternal sparkle of youth! And in this field of girls, a few boys, youths, men. Weak, narrow-chested (many in glasses), somehow deficient − understandably, otherwise they would have been in the war. Among these boys, one attracted her attention for some reason, probably because he seemed healthier than the others. Thin, tall even sitting down, with straight, light-blond hair and a dark-complexioned, irregular face, he looked up at her with the mocking triumph of youth and strength. He wore a faded military shirt with the shoulder straps removed, and his eyes were the same khaki color, large and gay almost to the point of impertinence. You couldn't just say about these eyes that they were laughing; no, they were laughing out loud, they were roaring with laughter. It seemed that he was controlling himself with difficulty: she need only leave the class room and he would let himself go. Then all these pale girls and eye-glassed boys would start giggling and roaring with laughter. Sometimes before the lecture, standing outside the door, she would even hear this group laughter that died down when she entered. Of course, it was clear who was boss here! In his own way he was as much a master of his art as she was of hers: he also knew how to command the attention of others, but his skill was loftier, because its source was not sterness but joy. Coming into the

58

classroom, she soon got used to looking for the laughing, khaki eyes, even to competing with him visually: Who would win? He would merrily look up, and at the same time down, at her. Who was she to the youth of this twenty-year-old? a learned woman, no longer young, probably boring, from whom one could always expect something unpleasant: she could call you to the blackboard, give you an F. . . . She would look at him with enmity: young, strong, here he sits with the girls and eye-glassed, narrow-chested boys, laughing with his eyes. . . . But once, when she actually did call him to the blackboard, she saw with what difficulty he got up after somehow moving aside his unbending leg. Only then did she notice two stripes on his khaki sleeve — one red and one yellow — and she reproached herself.

. . . So even then he was somehow marked for her? Or maybe it only seemed that way now. Because those same khaki eyes had looked at her today under the bouncing street lamp. Except that they had been laughing then, while today, in the impending darkness, they were full of suffering, out of focus. But then these eyes went back into focus for a moment and became harsh. This was when he had crushed the maple leaf with his foot: "I couldn't care less about that." How harshly he had said this: "I couldn't care less about that." So he did somewhat care about it after all?

She didn't know that much about him. They met again, after the Urals, last year: she had been a widow about two years. He worked in the same field as she, and a shared scientific topic connected him with her institute. It was a cost-accounting topic, a lot of trouble. Not many people knew him here, even the typists, and they always know everyone. What was said about him was that he was a promising young scientist. He wasn't all that young. They said that he was married but for some reason not living with his wife. Apparently she had left him for someone else and took the child, a girl, with her. Someone even knew the girl's name: Pashenka. And that was all. He hadn't changed much since those days. His lameness was barely noticeable now — only something hopping, amusing in his walk. No, he had changed after all: his hair was thinner, as if it had melted and moved back; knots of some kind had appeared on the muscles of his cheek-bones. But most of all his eyes had changed — they didn't laugh as often now. . . . But when they did — what they did to people! Weekdays disappeared and turned into holidays. Everything became interesting, special. And he showed off: Look at what the world can be and you don't notice, but I'll show you. See? It's me. I'm inviting you to a feast, so laugh. When he would come to the lab with such a face, everything would change, everything would be drawn to him. The gloomy, gray professor with a wart on his cheek would perk up his ear like a dog and wait. The old lab technician in a brown lab coat with a worn-out face and blotches from the reagents on her thin, work-worn hands, the lab assistant with pigtails like Katya's — everyone woke up and looked forward to the laughter, and the laughter came and they laughted and were happy. Tatiana Vasilievna laughed along with the others. Now she could laugh with him, not like then, in the classroom, where he had only waited for her departure to begin. In the evening, at home, she sometimes would remember that funny holiday and try to tell the children about it, but it never turned out. Apparently, it was not in the words, but in the tone, the voice, the eyes, who the hell knows, in what!

And then, more and more often it began to seem to her as though he was coming over and talking and showing off just for her alone. . . .

And she? Once, talking about him at home, she halted, feeling Katya's gaze on her. The straightforward gray eyes were asking point-blank: "Are you living correctly?" My dear Katya, how are you looking at me? Has it come to this alredy? Apparently so.

. . . And then, finally the black, autumn evening, the street lamp on the corner. . . .

. . . No, not about that. She had to leaf through the past, finally find that "warm spot" that was still eluding her. To understand, finally, what was the image that was persecuting her all evening and by now half the night, saying: no, everything is not all right.

*   *   *

So, the war. The evacuation. The ceaseless pain inside her. It was the beginning of their second year in a strange city. Life was sometimes harder, sometimes easier; in general, more often easier, but how little strength there was.

Aunt Marie took ill. Actually, she had weakened long before, moving around the apartment less and less. But now she took to her bed entirely. Things became more difficult for Tatiana Vasilievna. Now every day when she got back from work, she had to tidy up Aunt Marie, lifting her up on the bed with effort and changing the poor rags that used to be sheets under her. And there was no water. Tatiana Vasilievna controlled herself; she never allowed herself to get annoyed and did everything patiently, attentively, but without pity, with a stone heart. Where was she to get warm feelings for Aunt Marie as well? It was simply unfair, nobody would dare demand that of her. She hadn't particularly liked Aunt Marie even before this. What could she do? Just look after her, wash her, and feed her, but not love her, no, for this she did not have the strength. Once, when she was lifting Aunt Marie up on bed, suddenly two bony arms embrased her and she felt a kiss on her cheek. This was terrible. Oh, with what power love and pity came alive somewhere out there! But she did not let them get to her. No, she could not love Aunt Marie, too, for this she didn't have enough spiritual strength.

And then, one evening when she got home, she was struck by an unusual silence: Tolya and Volya were not fighting but silently going through some buttons in the corner, and Katya, looking very serious, was sitting at Aunt Marie's bedside. "Mama, something's happened to Aunt Marie, she's not talking," said Katya. "I took care of the boys and they're being quiet."

Tatiana Vasilievna walked up to the bed with mixed feelings. There was the timid, ignoble feeling of relief (could this be the end of my torment?) and shame for this relief; there was also a cowardly thought, like a prayer: no, no, please, only not now, only don't let it be this time! But Aunt Marie was alive. Her face was dark red and her breathing was rasping and difficult. They took her temperature — it was 102.2. The doctor diagnosed pneumonia and ordered her hospitalized the next day.

The next morning the ambulance came and Aunt Marie was taken to the hospital. She was still unconscious. Tatiana Vasilievna walked with the stretcher down to the car and kissed the wan, hot forehead good-bye. Suddenly the eye, the crossed one, opened and Aunt Marie said in French, completely clearly and even in a hearty voice: "au revoir."

They tidied up Aunt Marie's corner, covered the bed with a white piqué blanket, and the room immediately looked brighter. The little Tolya-Volya engine started running. Katya cried for a while and then quieted down.

That night Tatiana Vasilievna didn't sleep, A burning, abundant pity, finally having penetrated all barriers, flooded over her from the inside. She imagined how lonely and frightening it was for Aunt Marie there in the hospital, she didn't have anything with her, not even that packet. . . . Poor Aunt Marie, nobody had ever loved her, nobody had ever needed her. But now she was needed, oh, so needed, if she only knew! When she dies, Tatiana Vasilievna will be left all alone – the oldest member of the family. While Aunt Marie was around, she could allow herself to feel a little like a girl. But now – an adult, the eldest, forever. How awful! And she promised herself: If only Aunt Marie would get better, if only she would get better, I will always love and pity her the way I do now.

In the morning she called the information desk at the hospital. "I'll go and find out," answered a fresh and cheerful, apparently young, girlish voice. A long moment passed. "Who's asking for her?" the girl asked, in a different voice this time.

"A relative."

"A close relative?"

"No, not very (very close, very close, screamed a voice in her soul)."

"Well then, your old lady died yesterday. After they brought her here, washed her, fixed her up, then she died. It's okay, she died peacefully, properly. It's better for you this way. She would have been chronically ill, who would have kept her in the hospital."

. . . So. Aunt Marie died. This still had to be comprehended. She therefore no longer had to love and pity her as she had been planning to last night. She had to bury her.

A busy day passed. The coffin was ordered, the dress, kerchief, and shoes were ready, the cemetery plot was bought. Tomorrow would be Sunday. The funeral would be tomorrow.

That night Tatiana Vasilievna again lay sleepless, having set the alarm so as not to oversleep. The pity and love that had been tearing her apart the night before had quieted down now, but she still couldn't sleep. The alarm clock ticked, rushing and choking, and it seemed to her that this was time itself that was crowding her, crowding her and forcing her out of life. While there, in the hospital, Aunt Marie, whom everyone had already forced out, lay dead and cold.

Tomorrow came. That Sunday was impossible to forget. It was

already October, even late October, but the day turned out sunny and quiet, festive somehow. In the almost-warm, almost-summery sunlight, the trees were almost entirely bare, with only occassional sparkling yellow and red leaves. The whole city was light, bright, and amazingly quiet. The hospital garden was also quiet and amazing. It was completely empty, and the trees still modestly quiet, with their thin, black branches raised to the sun. In the far corner of the garden, Tatiana Vasilievna found a small building, like a chapel, which she recognized by the cross on the pediment to be the mortuary. She entered a small hall, where two bodies were lying properly and somehow peacefully on two raised platforms: one in a coffin, the other without. She went out into the garden to look for someone. In another corner of the garden an old woman in a gray quilted jacket, felt boots, and a gray scarf was gathering yellow leaves into a bag. Tatiana Vasilievna walked up to her; the woman looked up with curiosity and used the back of her hand to fix the scarf that had gone awry. Her hand was covered with soil. The garden smelled of the soil and fallen leaves. Instead of taking care of her own business, Tatiana Vasilievna for some reason asked, looking at the leaves:

"Why are you gathering them?"

"To heat with," the old woman said; she smiled and suddenly turned young — about thirty, no more. They both stood there smiling at each other.

"Excuse me," said Tatiana Vasilievna, selecting her words with difficulty, "could you tell me where the manager is here, that is, someone, you know, who'd be in charge of the mortuary?"

"The mortuary?" The woman looked merrily at her. She didn't understand a thing.

"You know," said Tatiana Vasilievna, "here's my problem: My aunt died in the hospital, and I want to bury her today, so, well, from whom do I get permission or whatever for this. . . .

This time, apparently, the woman caught on. The merry bewilderment on her face flared up even brighter.

"What am I saying," she said, "of course I have them all. They're all mine. Take her, take your departed."

"I would like to know what formalities are required, what papers I'm supposed to give you, what certificate, for example."

"Certificate?" the woman caught on and laughed. She laughed with relish and wiped the tears from her face with the back of her hand. "What on earth do I need a certificate for? Take her, take them all if you want. Some goods she's found. Oh, I almost died laughing."

After she had her laugh, she took Tatiana Vasilievna to the morgue – as they said around here, the "caterary." Walking behind her, Tatiana Vasilievna wondered where this strange word had come from. Maybe from the French, "cadavre" – corpse. . . . "Cadaverery." Along the way the woman managed to report everything about herself: four children, husband fighting, life was hard, but things were okay, really, she got tags for the children, the work was clean here in the caterary, only it didn't pay well, but then, her relatives were thankful – her relatives' departed ones, that is to say, some needed washing, some needed dressing, before you knew it they looked quite alive. Tatiana Vasilievna became silently absorbed in the aching, dizzying feeling inside her: she was about to go into the morgue to identify Aunt Marie from among the bodies.

In the basement, on unpainted wooden tables lay three corpses: two male and one female. Tatiana Vasilievna somehow didn't expect them to be lying there completely naked. She didn't exactly expect them to be dressed, but she didn't expect them to be naked. But they were naked and were lying on their backs and the female one – the old-womanish one – was Aunt Marie. Her hair had been shaven close to her head and she didn't resemble herself at all. Tatiana Vasilievna silently pointed her out to the watchwoman. For a moment she felt ill, the walls floated off to the side, but she pulled herself together and went out. In the small hall with the two bodies – how beautiful they were, dressed and quiet – she gave the watchwoman the bag with the clothing and a loaf of bread – for dressing Aunt Marie and putting her in the coffin. The watchwoman was glad. She merrily assured her that everything would be done just right, that yesterday she had fixed up and dressed a body so well – like a doll. Tatiana Vasilievna was also glad. So as not to see Aunt Marie naked anymore, she would have agreed not to eat bread for a month. But still she was ashamed – she had given away the bread, taken fright. And it wasn't even her bread – the boys' milk. She went home, exhausted from pangs of conscience, but still relieved. There were still three hours left until the funeral. She decided to go to a flower shop and try to get at least a few flowers there.

At home she suggested to Katya: "Do you want to come to the flower shop with me and buy some flowers for Aunt Marie?" And little Katya, as if she, too, were exhausted from pangs of conscience, put her thin, cool fingers into her mother's hand.


They were walking to the flower shop — by what miracle had it survived during war-time? — and the sun shone on them. The improbable, fine, and clear summer Sunday in October was continuing. The huge lot of the flower shop — apparently also in honor of Sunday — was completely deserted and empty. They went into the greenhouse. There, in the slanting rays of the sun with dancing bits of dust, sat a fat woman, crying noiselessly. The tears seemed to fall not from her eyes, but all at once from every pore of her flabby face. She gave no answer to the question: can one buy some flowers here? She just continued to cry, wiping her face with the hem of her jacket. It was strange, like in a fairy-tale, even frightening — the silence, the sun, and the noiselessly crying woman. There were no flowers in the greenhouse. Tatiana Vasilievna quietly closed the door behing her and took Katya by the hand: "Let's go and see if there's any greenery left in the flowerbeds." And she and Katya moved along the flowerbeds. Of course, there were neither flowers nor greenery. On the black earth, in places velvety-bluish-gray from the night's frost, lay only dead, frozen stalks and brown potato lashes. Everything was dead and black in the light of the sun. Tatiana Vasilievna had just decided to go back home, when they suddenly and unexpectedly found "it."

"It" was a small, yellow, poor little flower on a short stem, with a shaggy and anemic corolla, and it wasn't so much standing as lying in the flowerbed, and the corolla was slightly blackened on one side from the frost. Why had it bloomed? Had it made a mistake, taking fall to be spring? It lay there and seemed to be waiting for them, touching and out of place. Tatiana Vasilievna took it and later placed it on the coffin, on Aunt Marie's chest.

And that was all.

So there it was, finally, that importunate, elusive memory! Finally she understood what image had been tormenting her all evening, all night. It was "it" — the small, yellow flower, placed on the chest of an ugly, dead old woman and nailed shut with her in the coffin.

The alarm clock went off. Tatiana Vasilievna stretched out her hand and pushed down the button. The alarm clock went silent. It was gray in the room, rain slid along the window.

The alarm clock. Morning. She had to get up and get going.

*Translated by Dobrochna Dyrcz-Freeman*

Natalia Baranskaya

# THE RETIREMENT PARTY

The ceremony was taking place in the auditorium. The narrow auditorium was almost empty. Some twenty people sat in the first rows, and three on stage. The stage was separated from the auditorium by an arch of three red calico curtains. White diamond patterns wound around them. Under the arch was a table with a plush tablecloth, a carafe and a pale pink hydrangea in a flowerpot. At the table sat a broad-shouldered man with an affable face — the director — and a heavy young woman in a bright green jumper — the union representative.

Nearby, in an old office armchair, sat a thin homely woman with deep-sunken eyes and a halo of permanent over her bulbous forehead. She sat erect, unmoving; only her thin hands twisted and untwisted a handkerchief.

They were celebrating Anna Vasilevna Kosova's retirement. The entire bookkeeping staff was assembled, as well as several of the oldest workers in the company — everyone who knew her. She was mild-mannered, taciturn, and had sat for almost twenty years hunched over the records, abacus and accounts on her desk. There weren't many who knew her.

The union representative spoke first. She said that comrade Kosova was one of the most senior workers in the company, always distinguished for her diligence, never late, never needed to be disciplined, in fact had received two commendations, and that it was from workers like her that one could learn a conscientious attitude towards work.

"You are leaving for a deserved rest, comrade Kosova," she concluded. "And we hope it goes well for you. The administration and the union extend their official gratitude for your long years of honest service, and your comrades tender you this precious gift."

and she lifted a sheet of paper covering six teacups painted in yellow and violet.

There was scattered clapping. Anna Vasilevna raised her handkerchief to her lips and began to blink, suppressing the tears she had long been on the brink of.

The director raised a pudgy hand with a wedding ring on it. He asked for attention. He rose, and leaning on the table, spoke quietly, in a mild voice:

"Dear comrade Kosova, today we are sending you off to a deserved rest, as was rightly said. You have been spoken of as a good worker. I would like to add some words about you as a person." He paused a moment and continued: "You worked in the company twenty years — more precisely twenty-one years and eight months. I came here, as you know, two years ago. In the years that you have worked as an accountant, there have been four directors. What does that speak of, comrades? It speaks of the enviable human quality of Anna. . ." ("Vasilevna," the union representative prompted), "Yes, Anna Vasilevna, of her constancy."

He looked around the auditorium at the attentive faces and continued:

"Believe me, it's hard to part with such a person, comrades, but in each of our lives, as they say, that fateful hour strikes. We aren't saying farewell, Anna Vasilevna, we're saying 'till we meet again.' We hope to still work with you from time to time, at our mutual need."

He concluded to loud, friendly applause. Anna Vasilevna's lips trembled, and for a long time she pressed the handkerchief to her mouth. "How well they speak, and how well they all think of me," she thought, flustered. "I wish they'd finish, I can't take any more."

But the chief accountant asked to say a few words. He mounted the stage with difficulty, drew a handkerchief from his pocket, wiped his glasses, started to put them in his pocket, then put them on again over his large nose and said in his sad, soft voice:

"My esteemed Anna Vasilevna, we worked many, many years together. You are a very good worker. And a very, very good comrade. . . . He stopped, then added very softly: "excuse me, please," and returned to his seat.

Anna Vasilevna looked at him in alarm. But then a short-legged red-haired girl with a flushed, freckled face and carrot-colored curly hair jumped up on stage, shook her head, shot the director a quick look and shouted gaily to the auditorium:

"Our union committee invites you all to tea, on its own behalf. . . and Aunt Annie's, of course, so we ask you to come to the Accounting Office, all of you. . ." She looked at the director again, giggled, jumped down wiggling her thighs, and finished on the run: "The samovar won't boil, the teapot's tee'd out – bring the new cups, we don't have enough!"

Everyone got up, started to talk all at once, crowded around Anna Vasilevna and in a decorous procession with flowered cups and saucers in hand filed out of the auditorium.

The director excused himself on the way – business, he said – and went home. "That redhead is hot," he thought, grinning.

Tea didn't last long. The women glanced at the clock and at their bags filled with things they'd bought during dinner break. Anna Vasilevna wanted to go home too. She was tired and hot in her woolen off-duty dress. They hurriedly rinsed out cups, packed the new ones in the cake box, took "Bologna" coats from the coatrack. They went outside together, then began to say goodbye. Some went left, others straight across to the streetcar stop. Anna Vasilevna went right.

Her friend Marya Petrovna went with her. They had known each other a long time. They worked in a sewing shop during the war, sewing quilted jackets for the army. They had both been soldiers. And in the same year they both lost their husbands. Panteleeva was left with two children, Kosova with one. The former had grandchildren now, the latter had nobody.

"Don't get upset, Nyura," said Marya Petrovna, looking into her friend's sunken eyes. "Think of your health."

"What good is it to anyone, my health," Anna Vasilevna replied.

"What can you do, it's all in God's hands."

Anna Vasilevna only sighed in reply. She didn't believe in God. In that terrible year when both had been felled by grief, Maria Petrovna found consolation in the church. Anna Vasilevna didn't.

69

She healed herself with work.

She loved her uncomplicated profession. She never talked about it. What was there to talk about? It was funny. She simply never complained, never moaned like the others, never cursed her humble lot. She worked eagerly, adroitly, efficiently. No one could more quickly discover an error, find some damned kopeck that everyone was in a fever about at the end of the quarter. And everybody constantly came to her with requests – to check, to finish, to help. She never refused. She worked, and that was it.

She worked until that year, that month, when she was fifty-eight years old. And today they had given her a retirement party, and she was going home for the last time. How did all this happen?

This is how it was. First Masha Panteleeva said, as she had heard secretly from the typist, that they wanted to retire her, that is, Kosova. Masha didn't know if it was true. The typist didn't say where she got this information. They talked about it, and calmed down a bit: people would blather about anything. Still, from that day on, something came over Anna Vasilevna – she felt tight inside and couldn't breathe easily. When the union representative Antonina Rozhnova called her, she thought: "Well, so it's true," and her heart started to beat, and her throat was tight.

Rozhnova asked Anna Vasilevna how many years she had worked in the company, then inquired about her length of service as a whole. Anna Vasilevna began to count and counted almost forty years, maybe even forty-one. She was still a girl when she started working. The conversation proceeded in a casual way, as if Rozhnova was simply interested in Anna Vasilevna as a co-worker. Then all at once Antonina said:

"Comrade Kosova, the administration suggested that I clarify some questions concerning you, since there is a feeling that you ought to be recommended for retirement."

"What, Tonya, do I work any worse than the young ones? As far as I know no one's complained about me."

"No one's suggesting that you work any worse. You're just a lot older. They haven't reached retirement age, and you have."

"Then why do I have to leave, if I don't work any worse than they do, explain to me, Tonya?"

"Well what in the world do you want me to say?" Rozhnova flared up. "I didn't say you were worse. We aren't even comparing at all whether you work better or worse. We're talking about something else entirely. You've worked forty years, while the others, the younger ones, haven't yet. So give them a chance to work too."

In the face of this argument, as irresistible as a gravestone, Anna Vasilevna was silent. What could she say in reply to it? Antonina was probably right. Still, she expressed her desire to speak with the chief accountant – he understood her work.

"Don't make him go against regulations, Kosova. You can see the man can barely walk, he's clutching at his heart. Of course it's your right to talk to the administration. By the way, the director said: 'If she – meaning you – doesn't want to submit her request, bring her to me.' You may not agree with him, you may even have a grievance with him, but personally I wouldn't advise raising a ruckus."

Anna Vasilevna went back to her desk in accounting, wrote a request and took it right away to personnel. That was two weeks ago.

Three went to the left – the chief accountant Yakov Moiseevich Zuskin, the accountant Lyudmila Kharitonova and the bookkeeper Lelka Morkovkina. Lyudmila, calm and thorough, never hurried, while the redhead Lelka, or Carrot-top Lelka, was always in a rush, always late, always running. Now it was costing her a great effort to walk along with her companions. But today was a special day, and she felt sorry for Yakov Moiseevich: the old man was thoroughly out of sorts, that was a fact. Lelka listened out of one ear to his complaint and Kharitonova's sympathetic yeses, while she avidly thought over her own affairs.

"It'll be fine if Yurka has already run after Alka in the garden. But what if Yurka forgot about it playing? Which would be better – to look around the courtyards for Yurka or to run after Alka myself? I can make dinner in a jiffy: fry some chops, boil some noodles – it'll only take a minute. Benjamin isn't playing tonight, I think. Or maybe he is? Is he or isn't he? I forget . . . my memory's going! The fact is, I won't have time to iron him a white shirt. It's awful, the way he sweats at work! And they keep on saying: "Some job – blowing a trumpet!' They ought to try blowing one themselves. . . . There'll be hell to pay if I don't have a shirt ready!"

Lelka's husband tormented her with two passions — clean shirts and jealousy. She cursed the first and welcomed the second. Jealousy wafted her an air of romance over the horror of everyday life. Lelka remembered the director. She would have to tell Benny about his syrupy glance. . . and how afterwards . . . when they were serving tea, the director put his hand on the back of her chair and whispered to her: "Pour me some tea — it's sweeter from your hands. . ." No, not that. "In your hands tea turns into wine. . . ." Or maybe: "Your tea makes me drunk when I look at you." Aha, that was it!

Finally, her corner! Still, on parting she tried to comfort Yakov Moiseevich:

"It won't help for you to carry on about Anna Vasilevna like someone who's died. It's not even good. A person has retired. . . why, that's happiness! If right now I was given fifty rubles and told: 'You're free, comrade Morkovkina,' why, I'd. . . ."

Don't talk nonsense," Lyudmila interrupted her, "We'd do better to arrange with the whole accounting office to go visit her next week."

"Sure," Lelka said cheerfully. "See you later."

Soon Kharitonova turned off as well. Yakov Moiseevich went on. As soon as he was alone, his thoughts returned to that day in May.

Right after the May holidays the director of the company Shavrov called Yakov Moiseevich in.

"Good day, Yakov Moiseevich," the director greeted him, extending his hand and pushing a silver cigarette case towards him. "Have a smoke!"

"Thank you, Pavel Romanovich, I don't smoke," answered Yakov Moiseevich, touching two fingers to the left side of his chest, which meant, his heart wouldn't allow it.

"I wanted to ask you, Yakov Moiseevich, are there any employees of retirement age in the accounting office? Naturally I don't mean you." The director smiled; he was joking. The company couldn't do without Yakov Moiseevich; the director himself called him "the high-flying accountant."

"So what about the old ladies in your harem, eh?"

Yakov Moiseevich averted his eyes. He didn't want to talk about that. He tried to joke his way out of it.

"They're all young in my harem, the old ones are even younger than the young ones," he said despondently.

But the director was no longer disposed to joke. Glancing at some sheet of paper, he got down to business:

"You have a bookkeeper named Kosova, born in 1907. I think it's time she had a rest. "What's her salary, seventy? Well, she'll lose a little, fifteen or eighteen rubles."

"She's a good worker," the chief accountant rejoined.

"We don't have any other kind, if I know you. And if we do, let's get rid of them. Is there someone in particular we could do without?"

Yakov Moiseevich was silent.

"Well, we'll just have to grin and bear it," the director said soothingly. "As far as I can see, Kosova is the most suitable candidate. It's time she had a rest! She can bake pies for her old man, look after her grandchildren."

"Her husband died in the war."

"And how long ago was that! The war has been over for twenty years. She must have found another one ages ago."

"She doesn't have anybody. Neither children nor grandchildren. And she's a good worker, an excellent worker."

"Please, Yakov Moiseevich, don't let's quarrel." Shavrov began to drum his fingers on the table. Everyone in the company knew this sign of oncoming irritation. "How does the song go? Our young will always have a way, our old are honored everywhere.' We have to break in new staff."

Yakov Moiseevich asked if the director had a specific candidate in mind.

"We'll see, we'll see," Shavrov answered distractedly, leafing through the papers in his folder. "So, are we agreed?"

"I don't want to hurt a good person," Yakov Moiseevich sighed.

"Don't hurt her, then; throw her the finest party, give her a nice gift. . . . The director took out a zippered purse and rustled some bills. "Here," he said, taking a three-ruble note. "No wait, I have change." And he took a silver ruble out from under the bills.

"And see that you don't skimp, either."

"Not now," Yakov Moiseevich objected. "Let the union representative take care of that."

"All right, all right," the director agreed. "Things are agreed with you, for the rest you aren't needed. We'll talk to Kosova without you as well." And he dialed the number of the union representative.

"Hello? Rozhnova? This is Shavrov. Listen Tonya, do you know Kosova from accounting? She was born in 1907. How do you find her? Slow? You hear, Yakov Moiseevich, your Kosova is slow. Okay, okay, stop by my office, Rozhnova, we're having a conference. In ten minutes or so. That's all."

Yakov Moiseevich rose. He wanted terribly to put his hand on hes chest; his heart ached. But he restrained himself.

"Yes, Yakov Moiseevich, I've read your request. I'll talk it over with Rozhnova shortly. I want to accommodate you, but we can't forget about business either, of course."

This was a request for additional leave without pay. Yakov Moiseevich had long been waiting for a decision.

"Oh, how unpleasant, how bad," thought the chief accountant, descending the steps. "I've gotten old, really old."

And on his way he passed Rozhnova, smoothing her jumper, which was rising along her stout flanks.

Anna Vasilevna arrived home, sat down on a chair and sat for a long time without moving or thinking of anything. Afterwards she felt like having potatoes with green onion. She hadn't eaten since morning. She hadn't even been able to eat the cake — her stomach was too upset.

Anna Vasilevna took off her good dress, put on a robe and went into the kitchen. It was empty there. She was overjoyed: she didn't feel like talking. Anna Vasilevna ate, drank tea and washed the dishes. She thought about darning socks or reading a newspaper, but she was so sleepy that she barely had the energy to make the bed.

She lay down on her old bed with the sagging springs, put out the light, settled herself more comfortably on her right side and, sweetly sighing, closed her eyes. Through her head ran all sorts of trivialities, as always before sleep. Whether Carrot-top Lelka wouldn't forget to redo the account for payment of the trimmings. . . a burning smell was coming from the kitchen; that fat woman was always smoking up the apartment. . . where was her handkerchief? It wasn't in her bag — she must have lost it, too bad. . . . It would be interesting to know if Benjamin would be jealous tonight because Lelka was late. She'd tell about it tomorrow — a whole romance. . . .

But now it hit her like an electric shock — she wouldn't see Lelka tomorrow! She wouldn't be going to work tomorrow!

Anna Vasilevna tossed over on her back so that the springs nearly threw her on the floor. Anxieties — large and small — welled up in her. How would she live now? What would she do? How would she kill the time?

She hadn't mended her coat last year, she had gone on vacation. Now the coat was probably beyond her strength. If she set aside so much for food each day. . . and Anna Vasilevna began to think about her new budget. Then she was sorry that she hadn't saved money , she had spent it all. True, she never did have much to save. If earlier, when she had lived with her husband. . . but had they lived together long?

She had married late. She wouldn't have married at all, had she not met a man as modest, quiet and unsettled as herself. His first wife was disappointed in him because he didn't earn a good living, divorced him, sued him successfully for half a room, and afterwards drove him out altogether. He let a corner from the old woman in this very apartment. Anya lived then with her mother in the large room. At that time her room was only a piece out of the large one. The window was even somewhere in the corner.

She looked out the window — the sky was already getting light. She told herself sternly: "Better sleep, it's almost morning." But sleep didn't come.

In the predawn twilight Anna Vasilevna looked around at her room, as if she was seeing it for the first time. It was narrow and crooked. It was wider at the head, narrower at the feet. . . . "What is it, it's like a grave, really, it is." She was frightened. It seemed like the walls were pressing in, the ceiling was lowering onto her chest. It was hard to breathe. And there on a poplar under the window a crow woke up and cawed three times in a rusty voice.

"That's a bad omen, a very bad omen," She thought miserably.

She felt on the brink of tears again. But her thoughts again kept her from crying. She remembered the last wearisome days.

In the accounting office they had talked a lot about Anna Vasilevna's leaving, made various speculations, pitied her, tacitly blamed Yakov Moiseevich and cursed Rozhnova. At first this made Anna Vasilevna feel better, as if the hurt were beginning to pass away. But these conversations quickly became unbearable to her – she was heartsick. There was still time left – let the days not pass, that was all.

Later everyone got tired of feeling sorry for Anna Vasilevna, and talked about the other one – whoever it was God would send them.

"The administration knows who God will send," Lelka giggled.

They began to think and guess what she would be like, the new co-worker. "Most likely some hoity-toity," said Kharitonova. Lelka began to picture her, this future hoity-toity. She made her lips into a trumpet, forcing her words through them, lisping, walking without bending her knees, on tiptoe, figured the account splaying her fingers out, and said, sadly rolling her eyes: "We have a total of a million kopeks and a hundred thousand rubles." Everyone laughed; things were never boring with Lelka around. But Anna Vasilevna's heart ached. They were already forgetting about her.

She fell asleep in the early morning. The top of the poplar was lit – the sun was up. The birds woke, the yard was filled with twittering, singing, chirping. Loud sounds were heard, a child's crying, and somewhere the roar of a motorcycle. A woman shouted impatiently: "Vanya, are you coming?" People were going to work. Anna Vasilevna slept.

She was awakened by a loud ringing. The alarm clock had gone off – cheerfully, desperately, knocking its metal legs on the table and slowly turning its round body.

"Are you out of your mind?" She asked it tenderly, in a sleepy voice. She never set the alarm; she always woke up on time. But the hands already pointed to eight o'clock. "I'm late?!" she groaned and quickly sat up, immediately sliding her feet into her slippers.

And only then did she remember: she didn't have to go anywhere. There was no need to get up. There was no need to do anything.

She sat on the edge of the bed, with her hands hanging limp.
The alarm clock rang and rang. It seemed as though that useless
sound would never end.

*Translated by Alan Shaw*

Marina Rachko

# NORTH OF RUSSIA

This time I was sent on assignment by the Pioneers' journal to write a piece about a progressive collective farm near Novgorod for young students. Why not about old Novgorod? Why not about the popular assemblies, the fistfights and the oprichniki? I didn't ask any of this, of course. As we're fond of saying, "you should have asked that in 1917".

It was early spring, bare as yet of any grass or greenery. The area around Novgorod is flat, and the water of innumerable lakes stands motionless on a level with the land. And over it a multitude of ancient white churches, always in two images – the real and the reflected.

I was driven from Novgorod to the collective farm in the district committee's car; my driver was getting on in years. I was ashamed to tear him and his car away from his trivialities for the sake of my own, and thereby join in the generally accepted system of trivialities and stupidities. But the bus went only along the other side of the Volkhov.

"How do the farm workers get to town?"

"They come across the river mouth by boat. They have a truck, too, if they need it."

We went the whole way tire-deep in red clayey mud, afraid every moment of getting stuck. But the driver was a real "ace" and we made it through safe and sound. As I took my leave of him I said:

"I never would have thought you could get such a classy ride through such mud."

The driver answered without the slightest theatricality:

"My dear, I was born and raised in the mud."

The village looked well-off, but very bleak. It stood on the boundary between the red mud and the pink water, and in the whole village there was only one large tree, on a little island.

First they brought me to the huge, cavernous brick school. The children were animated, and avid talkers. I asked them whether

78

anyone could drive a tractor, did they drown kittens, had they been to the theatre, did they want to go to the city, what would they advise me to take pictures of as being the most interesting or beautiful, had any among them drowned, what would they like to brag about, what was the scariest thing they could remember in their life . . . The children vied with their answers. But there was nothing spirited in them. Not a spark of originality. I was sweating but my notepad remained empty. The reaction of the children to a reporter from the Pioneers' journal was instinctive and lightning-like: to say what was usually printed in the newspapers and journals. Their conventional responses didn't even contain funny mistakes or the accidental charms of local dialect. Nobody had specially taught them, they simply imbibed it with their mothers' milk, the milk of mothers born in 1937.

I tried to talk with the adults. But it was as if a numbness had come over the peasants. They only smiled, looking past me, and their eyes reflected their twilight-pink, sky-and-water solaris. Only one old girl made me laugh. I honestly admired her luxurious, extensive flowerbeds. She was looking intently at my coat and purse. Finally I said that at home, on my balcony in the city, I grew flowers as well; it was an activity I was very fond of. The old girl looked into the distance and said in a indefinitely sarcastic tone:

"Those activities are shit."

Only the chairman was full of enthusiasm, and it didn't seemed to be all for show, either.

"For six months I've been trying to talk some of these old women into moving into town houses, with all the conveniences . . . one is ashamed to show people your cottages, I tell them . . . No, they dug in their heels like rams."

In the room where the conversation was taking place there was, besides me and the chairman, a party organizer and a youngish teacher, who looked like a bleached Estonian boy. The party organizer sat on the edge of the table and stared out the window, entranced, at the water. Every time the chairman turned to him for approval, he began to stir, turning his eyes from the water with visible effort . . . And each time the chairman continued without waiting for his reaction. The teacher, in contrast to the chairman and the party organizer, was not in a quilted jacket, but in a black suit with white shirt and tie. As soon as the chairman finished, the teacher hurriedly invited me to spend the night at his apartment. He and his family lived in the very thing that was the chairman's pride – a town house.


The four-story house rose between the water and the mud, approached by wooden walkways. When we went inside, the smell of river water and spring mud was replaced by the familiar smell of a city entrance hall: a chill dampness and cat's urine. In the windows on the stairway landings the pink and lilac water and sky seemed to flow right up against the glass. As we went upstairs, several times a sudden rumbling was heard, as if the house were starting to crumble. It was children, stamping their boots and running on the stairs.

In the apartment we were met silently and without any special curiosity by a peasant woman with a restless, depressed face and a three-year-old girl who so smelled of piss that you couldn't hold her. Her beautiful young mother, who was in charge of the club, came in later and she, too said not a word the whole evening.

One room in the apartment was furnished according to city standards: bookshelves, cupboard, sofa bed and floor lamp. While in the second room and in the kitchen there was only a scattering of junk, giving it neither the neat appearance of a city apartment nor the coziness of a cottage. There was a sewer system, but it didn't work, so they used a bucket. There was running water as well, but all that came out of the faucet were rusty drops. So water was brought up from the well.

Since the whole family was stubbornly and impassively silent, I talked only with the girl, who was very bright.

Late that evening the teacher took an expensive brandy from the cabinet and gave some special nod of his boyish head. Instantly all his women disappeared, and after that I didn't hear a sound from behind the door.

I looked at the teacher. His face had taken on the look of a junky who was about to fall into convulsions if he didn't get his fix. I wasn't particularly frightened, since he was after all quite delicate compared to me, but I nevertheless prepared to put up a resistance. But the teacher had nothing of the sort in mind. He swallowed and said in a ravenous voice:

"Tell me about everything."

I somehow guessed immediately that he was simply tormented by spiritual thirst. Shaking off with an effort the hypnotic somnolence emanating from the window, I began to tell him. I told about the ferment of minds among the literary people and the educated. I told about the sudden outbreak of religiosity among the intelligentsia. About the young priest near Suzdal, whose sermons crowds of city intellectuals flocked to hear. About the craze for literature, and especially poetry, in the capitals.

Then I began to recite verses.

The times are not a thing one chooses;
One lives and dies in them.
There's nothing in the world more tasteless
Than whining and complaining.
As though you could reade this batch for that,
Like at the market.

The teacher grew radiant, his hair became dishevelled, and perspiration broke out on his forehead . . . As for myself, I could't stop.

It was easy to see what he wanted. He wanted to hear about himself and his generation, he wanted the pain and self-pity . . . and he didn't want it to be like the classics, which he himself, wrapped in his soviet packaging, drummed into his students' heads . . . he wanted it to be comprehensible, to go straight to the heart . . .

Drive me to Ostankino, chief,
To Ostankino, where the Titan cinema is.
She's working as a ticket-taker there;
Standing at the door all frozen,
All frozen and shivering,
But overcoming her love.
Understanding, grasping everything.
But never betraying and never forgiving.

I read and read, mixing up poets, adding bits of my own when I forgot. Towards the end I no longer knew what I was saying. The teacher left only after my head had begun to fall on my breast like a drunk woman's. There were two hours left for sleeping. Through the window the water and sky continually changed color, but night and darkness still didn't come.

*  *  *

In the morning the chairman and the party organizer, who was just
as torpid as the day before, took me to another village. Once more to
a school, only this time an elementary school.

"Why should I go to the school? I've been there already."

The chairman shushed me.

"No, there's a man there, a Distinguished Teacher. It's likely he'll
be a deputy soon. There's no getting out of it."

But the school unexpectedly got to me. It was housed in a large
cottage with a painted wooden floor, clean and pitiably bare. It was
in the midst of an apple orchard in a little out-of-the-way village
called "Chalovnitsa." In the hall on a rack there were five little
overcoats, and under them, five pairs of rubber boots. There was a
wash-stand over a basin and next to it a clean towel.

In the tiny staff room there was a miniature globe and an
enormous wooden protractor on the table.

The Distinguished Teacher proved to be a little hunchback with a
calm and even handsome large face. A real "little Herr Friedemann"
of Chalovnitsa. His fivesome of bright-eyed students attended to
every twitch of his eyebrows, but it was evident that it was out of
reverence rather than fear. Fifteen years ago he and his students of
that time had planted this orchard around the school, and now he fed
his present ones apples at recess. The apples were stored the whole
winter in the school's cellar. Ten years ago they had planted a grove
on the bare band of the Volkhov. It had become a real little forest.

The hunchback went majestically with me and the children into the
grove and gave an exam there. First he questioned me. I couldn't
recognize the naked, scarcely yet budding trees, but his kids new
nearly all of them. By the color of the bark, the shape of the buds,
and the arrangement of the branches. They were in utter rapture that
I didn't know anything. They jumped around me, laughing under their
breath. They didn't dare do it aloud. Afterwards the teacher merely
pointed towards the school, and they all ran obediently and neatly
hung their coats up and set out their boots. I asked permission to
listen to the lesson from the hall.

"So what did Vladimir Ilyich Lenin tell us about this?" the
teacher's deep baritone rang out, "Kolya Sergeev will answer."

82

The childish, choked voice, on a single high note, pronounced meaninglessly:

"Vladimir Ilyich said that we must not ask alms . . . of nature . . ."

The teacher calmly corrected him and the child innocently prattled through the quotation.

At that I left quietly. The chairman and the party organizer were waiting for me, looking pensevely into an unfinished well.


On the square in front of the garage, behind a wire fence, stood an orange facility. As we appeared, from the bunch of peasants, one stood out, on whose face good looks and coarseness were engaged in a battle that coarseness was winning. He yelled from a distance:

"So then, chairman, blank blank, I went out (he meant he had gone out to work. After a binge, obviously) . . . And my truck, blank blank blank, is in the shop, blank blank. Not an ounce of work."

The chairman and party organizer hurriedly went to meet the peasant, telling me to wait on the bank by the boat. The chairman also spoke loudly from a distance, to the whole square:

"And who was it broke your truck, Grisha?"

And turning to a fat storekeeper who had come out onto the porch of her store to watch the duel, he asked in passing:

"Stepanna, wasn't it you that bashed his truck up on the gate?"

Stepanna's face remained impassive, only her fat quivered slightly with laughter. The last thing I heard, turning on the path, was one old woman from the silent crowd at the store asking her:

"Stepanna, when are you going to have some eggs to sell?"

Still looking at the chairman and the peasant, she said:

"I'll sit right down and lay you some."

In fifteen minutes or so the chairman and party organizer, who evidently were not to be parted that day, took me in the boat to the other side of the Volkhov to the bus station. Both their faces had red blotches on them after talking. The chairman rowed. On the river everything, as on the day before, was bright pink; the water shone and merged dizzyingly with the sky. In the middle of the river the chairman stopped to rest. There was an awkward silence. The party organizer unexpectedly asked, without taking his eyes from the water:

"You know what's our biggest trouble?"

83

"No."

"They drink themselves to death . . . and why? Every bath-house has got a washing machine . . . every man's got a motorcycle . . . the wages are like you won't find in any other town."

"Why do you think they drink?"

"I think they need religion," said the party organizer. The chairman wheezed and started rowing again.

I knew that such trustfulness demanded complicity, and I said that it wasn't yet known if all of us could find faith, even if we were allowed to believe. Perhaps one had to earn faith.

"And who has earned it?" asked the party organizer.

He paused on the bank, as if wanting to prolong the discussion, but the cautious chairman wouldn't let him.

"Come on, come on, you philosopher," he said, standing behind me and most likely winking at the party organizer not to forget himself.

We went along the dried-up meadow road. We went on and on, the birds sang, and I forgot what I was going for. Afrerwards I had to collect myself piece by piece.

*Translated by Alan Shaw*

Nadezhda Mandelshtam

# MEMOIRS

(English title *Hope Against Hope*)

## BORIS PASTERNAK

In his letter to Stalin, Bukharin added a postscript saying he had been visited by Pasternak, who was upset by the arrest of Mandelstam. The purpose of this postscript was clear: it was Bukharin's way of indicating to Stalin what the effect of M.'s arrest had been on public opinion. It was always necessary to personify "public opinion" in this way. You were allowed to talk of one particular individual being upset, but it was unthinkable to mention the existence of dissatisfaction among a whole section of the community — say, the intelligentsia, or "literary circles." No group has the right to its own opinion about some event or other. In matters of the kind there are fine points of etiquette which nobody can appreciate unless he has been in our shoes. Bukharin knew how to present things in the right way, and it was the postscript at the end of his letter that explained why Stalin chose to telephone Pasternak and not someone else.

Their conversation took place at the end of July, when M.'s sentence had already been commuted, and Pasternak told a lot of people about it — Ehrenburg, for instance, who was in Moscow at the time and whom he went to see the same day. But for some reason he said not a word about it to anyone directly involved — that is, to me, my brother Evgeni, or Akhmatova. True, on the same day he did ring Evgeni, who already knew about the revision of the sentence, but only to assure him that everything would be all right. He said no more than this, and Evgeni, thinking his words were simply an expression of his optimism, attached no particular importance to them. I myself only learned about Stalin's call to Pasternak several months later when I came to Moscow from Voronezh a second time after being ill with typhus and dysentery. In casual conversation Shengeli asked me whether I had heard the story about Stalin's telephone call to Pasternak, and whether there

85

was anything in it. Shengeli was convinced that it was just a figment of somebody's imagination if Pasternak himself had not told me anything about it. I decided, however, to go to the Volkhonka and see Pasternak, since there is never smoke (and what smoke!) without fire. Shengeli's story was confirmed down to the last detail. As he told me about the conversation, Pasternak reproduced everything said by Stalin and himself in direct speech. It was just the same as what Shengeli had told me – evidently Pasternak had told it to everybody in identical terms and the version going around Moscow was entirely accurate. This is how Pasternak told me the story:

Pasternak was called to the phone, having been told beforehand who wished to speak with him. He began by complaining that he couldn't hear at all well because he was speaking from a communal apartment and there were children making a noise in the corridor. The time had not yet come when such a complaint would have been taken as a request – to be granted by way of a miracle – for an immediate improvement in one's living conditions. It was simply that Pasternak began any telephone conversation with this complaint. Whenever he was talking on the phone to one of us, Akhmatova and I would quietly ask the other – whichever of us happened to be on the phone with him: "Has he stopped carrying on about the apartment yet?" He talked with Stalin just as he would have talked with any of us.

Stalin began by telling Pasternak that Mandelstam's case had been reviewed, and that everything would be all right. This was followed by a strange reproach: why hadn't Pasternak approached the writers' organizations, or him (Stalin), and why hadn't he tried to do something for Mandelstam: "If I were a poet and a poet friend of mine were in trouble, I would do anything to help him."

Pasternak's reply to this was: "The writers' organizations haven't bothered with cases like this since 1927, and if I hadn't tried to do something, you probably would never have heard about it." Pasternak went on to say something about the word "friend," trying to define more precisely the nature of his relations with M., which were not, of course, covered by the term "friendship." This digression was very much in Pasternak's style and had no relevance to the matter in hand. Stalin interrupted him: "But he's a genius, he's a genius, isn't he?" To this Pasternak replied: "But that's not the point." "What is it, then?" Stalin asked. Pasternak then said that he would like to meet him and have a talk. "About what?"

"About life and death," Pasternak replied. Stalin hung up. Pasternak tried to get him back, but could only reach a secretary. Stalin did not come to the phone again. Pasternak asked the secretary whether he could talk about this conversation or whether he should keep quiet about it. To his surprise, he was told he could talk about it as much as he liked — there was no need at all to make a secret of it. Stalin clearly wanted it to have the widest possible repercussions. A miracle is only a miracle, after all, if people stand in wonder before it.

Everybody could now clearly see what miracles Stalin was capable of, and it was to Pasternak that the honor had fallen not only of spreading the good tidings all over Moscow, but also of hearing a sermon in connection with it. The aim of the miracle was thus achieved: attention was diverted from the victim to the miracle-worker. It was extraordinarily symptomatic of the period that, in discussing the miracle, nobody thought to ask why Stalin should have rebuked Pasternak for not trying to save a friend and fellow poet while at the same time he was calmly sending his own friends and comrades to their death. Even Pasternak had not thought about this aspect, and he winced slightly when I raised it with him. My contemporaries took Stalin's sermon on friendship between poets completely at its face value and were ecstatic about a ruler who had shown such warmth of spirit. But M. and I couldn't help thinking of Lominadze, who was recalled to Moscow for his execution while we were in Tiflis talking with him about the possibility of M.'s staying there to work in the archives. And apart from Lominadze, there were all the others whose heads had rolled by this time. There were already very many, but even now people still stubbornly continue to reckon only from 1937, when Stalin supposedly went to the bad all of a sudden and began to destroy everybody.

Pasternak himself was very unhappy about his talk with Stalin, and to many people, including me, he lamented his failure to follow it up with a meeting. He was no longer worried about M., since he had complete faith in Stalin's word that he would be all right. This made him feel his own failure all the more keenly. Like many other people in our country, Pasternak was morbidly curious about the recluse in the Kremlin. Personally, I think it was lucky for him that he did not meet Stalin, but at the time all this happened there was a good deal we did not yet understand – we still had much to learn. This was another extraordinary feature of the times: why were people so dazzled by absolute rulers who promised to organize heaven on earth, whatever it might cost? Nowadays it would never occur to anyone to doubt that in their confrontation with Stalin it was M. and Pasternak who came out on the side of right, displaying both moral authority and a proper sense of history. But at the time Pasternak was very upset by his "failure" and himself told me that for a long time afterward he could not even write poetry. It would have been quite understandable if Pasternak had wanted, as it were, to touch the sores of the era with his own hands, and, as we know, he subsequently did so. But for this he had no need of any meetings with our rulers. At that time, however, I believe that Pasternak still regarded Stalin as the embodiment of the age, of history and of the future, and that he simply longed to see this living wonder at close quarters.

Rumors are now being spread that Pasternak lost his nerve during the talk with Stalin and disowned M. Not long before his final illness I ran into him on the street and he told me about this story. I suggested we both make a written record of his conversation, but he didn't want to. Perhaps things had now taken such a turn for him that he no longer had time for the past.

How can Pasternak possibly be accused of such a thing – paricularly since Stalin started off by telling him he had already exercised mercy? According to the present rumors, Stalin asked Pasternak to vouch for M., but Pasternak supposedly refused to do so. Nothing of this kind happened, and the question of it never even arose.

When I gave M. an account of the whole business, he was entirely happy with the way Pasternak had handled things, particularly with his remark about the writers' organizations not having bothered with cases like this since 1927. "He never said a truer word," M. said with a laugh. The only thing that upset him was that the conversation had taken place at all. "Why has Pasternak been dragged into this? I have to get out of it myself – he has nothing to do with it." Another comment of M.'s was: "He [Pasternak] was quite right to say that whether I'm a genius or not is beside the point. . . . Why is Stalin so afraid of genius? It's like a superstition with him. He thinks we might put a spell on him, like shamans. And yet another remark: "That poem of mine really must have made an impression, if he makes such a song and dance about commuting my sentence."

Incidentally, it's by no means certain how things might have ended if Pasternak had started praising M. to the skies as a genius – Stalin might have had M. killed off on the quiet, like Mikhoels, or at least have taken more drastic measures to see that his manuscripts were destroyed. I believe that they have survived only because of the constant attacks on M. as a "former poet" by his contemporaries in LEF and among the Symbolists. As a result, the authorities felt that M. had been so discredited and was such a has-been that they did not bother to track down his manuscripts and stamp them out completely. All they did was to burn whatever came into their hands – this, they thought, was quite enough. If they had been led to think more highly of M.'s poetry, neither his work nor I would have survived. It would have been a case, as they say, of scattering our ashes to the winds.

The version of the telephone call from Stalin that has been told abroad is completely absurd. According to accounts published there, M. supposedly read his poem at a party in Pasternak's apartment, after which the poor host was "summoned to the Kremlin and given hell." Every word of this shows a total ignorance of our life – though one might well ask how any outsider could be expected to have enough imagination to picture the extent of our bondage! Nobody would have dared to breathe a word against Stalin, let alone read a poem like that "at a party." This is the sort of thing that only a provocateur would do, but even a provocateur would scarcely have dared to recite a poem against Stalin at a party. And then, nobody was ever summoned to the Kremlin for questioning. One was invited to the Kremlin for gala receptions and the ceremonial award of decorations. The place for interrogations was the Lubianka, but Pasternak was not asked to go there in connection with M. Indeed, Pasternak came to no harm at all as a consequence of his talk with Stalin, and it is not necessary to feel sorry for him because of this particular episode. One final point: it so happens that we never visited Pasternak at his home, and we saw him only when he came to see us from time to time. This arrangement suited us very well.

## NIKOLAI TIKHONOV

Nikolai Tikhonov, the poet, always talked in loud, self-confident tones. He had great charm and, with his beguiling ways, was good at winning people over. His literary debut was greeted with joy by all those who spoke of him in such glowing terms as a man of the new generation, a wonderful story-teller — and every inch a soldier to boot. Even now many people are still captivated by him, not realizing what he later became. He was first brought to see us by Nikolai Chukovski, and M. took a liking to both of them. "See what a kind person Kornei Chukovski's son is," he said. About Tikhonov he said: "He's all right — though I have the feeling he's the sort who might come into your compartment in a train and say 'Let's see your papers, citizens!'" M. pronounced the phrase in the way it was spoken by the commanders of grain-requisition units during the Civil War when they came through trains looking for black-marketeers. Even so, M. also fell under Tikhonov's spell — but not for long. We saw Tikhonov in his true colors earlier than other people. I particularly remember the passionate conviction in his voice as he said to us: "Mandelstam will not live in Leningrad. We will not give him a room." This was after our return from Armenia, when we had nowhere to live and M. had asked the writers' organization to live in Leningrad in a privately rented room. He stubbornly repeated his previous statement: "Mandelstam will not live in Leningrad." I tried to find out whether he was saying this on his own initiative or on somebody else's instructions, but I could not get any sense out of him. If it was on instructions, it was difficult to account for the depth of feeling in his voice. Whatever the truth of the matter, it boded no good, and we returned to Moscow. What Tikhonov was trying to convey by his tone of voice was more or less as follows: "We all behave in the way expected of us, and who does Mandelstam think he is to carry on like this, not caring a damn for anybody, and then come and ask us for work and a place to live! He flouts all the rules, and we have to answer for him." From his own point of view, Tikhonov was quite right. In the eyes of someone so totally devoted to the regime M. was an anomaly, a harmful emanation of the past, a person for whom there was no room in a literature where places were allotted by higher authority.

By this time we had already gained some insight into Tikhonov. Not long before our conversation about a room and the right to live in Leningrad, we happened to meet him as he was coming out of the editorial offices of *Zvezda* with his pockets full of manuscripts that he had been asked to advise on. He patted his pockets and said: "Just like at the front . . ." We knew that Tikhonov was dominated by his memories of the Civil War, but we failed to see what connection there could be between his bulging pockets and the front line. He explained that there was now a "war" going on in literature and it appeared that he was applying himself to his very modest literary activities with all the dash which had once distinguished him as a soldier. All he had to do to feel he was fulfilling his revolutionary duty was to "kill" half a dozen hack novels, of the kind with which any editor's desk is always cluttered, and simultaneously expose their ideological shortcomings. Wasn't that war? Moreover, it was war without the usual risks, and he didn't have to go out marauding to furnish his apartment with the modest attributes of Soviet comfort. What was wrong with that?

"Just like at the front" was Tikhonov's favorite saying, but we occasionally heard him use other triumphant war cries. Once I had to go and see him in Moscow — it happened to be April 23, 1932, the day that RAPP fell, as we had learned from the newspapers in the morning. Tikhonov was staying in Herzen House — where we were living at the time — but he was in the "aristocratic" wing, with Pavlenko. The fall of RAPP had come as a complete surprise to everyone. I found Tikhonov and Pavlenko sitting over a bottle of wine, drinking toasts to "victory." "Down with RAPP and all its works!" Tikhonov was shouting, resourceful as ever. Pavlenko, who was a much cleverer man (and a much more terrifying one), said nothing.

"But," I said to Tikhonov, "I thought you were a friend of Averbakh." It was Pavlenko, not Tikhonov, who replied to this: "The war in literature has entered a new phase."

When we were in Voronezh, M. sent Tikhonov his poem about Kashchei and the Tomcat, hoping for some reason that he might be prompted by the lines about gold and precious stones to send some money to a penniless fellow poet in exile. Tikhonov immediately cabled that he would do everything he could. This was the last we were to hear from him (through Surkov) of this cable at the beginning of the sixties, when the Poets' Library was desperately looking for someone to write a preface to a volume of M.'s poetry which had been scheduled by the editors. One after another, the people approached had refused to write it — nobody wanted to assume any part of the responsibility for "resurrecting" Mandelstam. If Tikhonov had agreed to write it, the book would probably have come out a long time ago — it was then a propitious moment, just before the publication of Solzhenitsyn's *One Day in the Life of Ivan Denisovich.* Tikhonov would have been the ideal person to write the preface — the mere fact of his agreeing to would have protected the volume from attacks on it. Such attacks can be fatal right up to the moment of publication. Surkov tried to persuade him to do it, and reminded him of his cable promising to "do everything." But Tikhonov refused outright. "He has turned into a Chinese idol," I said to Surkov, who did not demur.

It is difficult to dismiss entirely the "young Kolia," the youth with the expansive gestures, as we had once known him. "Tikhonov and Lugovskoi," Akhmatova once said to me, "have never done a thing to help anyone, but, all the same, they are a little better than the rest." She also told me how in 1937 she had run into Tikhonov in Leningrad and they had walked along one of the embankments for half an hour or so. Tikhonov kept complaining about how terrible the times were: "He said what we were all saying" — this is the reason Akhmatova still has a soft spot for him. But she was also struck by the way he said it. When she came home, she could not remember a single word of what he had actually said about the terror: everything had been so skillfully camouflaged that even in talking with Akhmatova he had managed not to compromise himself. All he did was to complain in general terms, without saying a word out of place: no one could say that he wasn't highly disciplined! I do not think he can be put in the same category as Lugovskoi, who was a completely different type — he had been scared stiff at the front, never involved himself in the "literary war," and when he was drunk he could say all kinds of odd things. Tikhonov, on the other hand, has always been true to himself and the cause he serves. The last of the Mohicans will come to his funeral to pay military honors to this literary warrior who never forgot that the magazine *Zvezda* was also part of the front line.

They say that Tikhonov's wife used to make toys out of papier-maché. Tikhonov himself is a papier-maché figure — scarcely a good repository for values of any kind. I doubt whether he had any to change when he first appeared on the scene at the beginning of the twenties as one of the best representatives of the "new era."

ISAAC BABEL

I do not think Babel ever lived in any of the apartment buildings
reserved for writers, but always managed to find peculiar places of
his own. With great difficulty we tracked him down in a strange
house that must formerly have been a private villa. I have a vague
recollection that there were foreigners living in this house, and that
Babel rented rooms from them on the second floor. But perhaps he
just said so to astonish us − he was very fond of startling people
like this. At that time foreigners were avoided like the plague −
you could lose your head for the slightest contact with them. Who in
his right mind would have lived in the same house as foreigners? I
still remember my astonishment, and still cannot understand it.
Whenever we saw Babel he gave us something to be surprised about.

We told him our troubles, and during the whole of our long
conversation he listened with remarkable intentness. Everything
about Babel gave an impression of all-consuming curiosity − the
way he held his head, his mouth and chin, and particularly his eyes.
It is not often that one sees such undisguised curiosity in the eyes of
a grown-up. I had the feeling that Babel's main driving force was
the unbridled curiosity with which he scrutinized life and people.

With his usual ability to size things up, he was quick to decide
on the best course for us. "Go out to Kalinin," he said, "Erdman is
there − his old women just love him." This was Babel's cryptic way
of saying that all Erdman's female admirers would never have
allowed him to settle in a bad place. He also thought we might be
able to get some help from them − in finding a room there, for
instance. But Babel, as it turned out, had exaggerated Erdman's hold
over his "old women" − when we went to Kalinin, we found that
none of them lived out there with him, and that he had to come into
Moscow to see them.

Babel volunteered to get the money for our fare the next day,
and we then started talking about other things.

He told us he now spent all his time meeting militiamen and drinking with them. The previous evening he had been drinking with one of the chief militiamen of Moscow, who in his drunken state had declared that "he who lives by the sword shall perish by the sword." The chiefs of the militia, he said, were disappearing one after another and "today you're all right, but you don't know where you'll be tomorrow."

The word "militia" was of course a euphemism. We knew that Babel was really talking about Chekists. . .

M. asked him why he was so drawn to "militiamen": was it a desire to see what it was like in the exclusive store where the merchandise was death? Did he just want to touch it with his fingers? "No," Babel replied, "I don't want to touch it with my fingers – I just like to have a sniff and see what it smells like."

It was known that among the "militiamen" Babel visited was Yezhov himself. After the arrest of Babel, Katayev and Shklovski said he had visited Yezhov because he was so frightened, but that it hadn't saved him – Beria had had him arrested precisely on this account. I am convinced that Babel went to see Yezhov not out of cowardice but out of sheer curiosity – just to have a sniff and see what it smelled like.

The question "What will happen to us tomorrow?" was the chief topic of all our conversations. Babel, with his storyteller's gift, put it into the mouth of his "militiamen." M. was generally silent about it – he knew too well what awaited him.


## THE SHKLOVSKIS

In Moscow there was only one house to which an outcast could always go. If Victor and Vasilisa Shklovski happened not to be at home when M. and I called during our trips to the city in the months before his arrest, one of the children would run out to greet us: little Varia, who always had a piece of chocolate in her hand, the tall Vasia (the daughter of Vasilisa's sister Natalia), or Nikita, their gangling son, who liked to go out catching birds and was also a great stickler for the truth. Nobody had ever explained anything to them, but they always knew what they had to do: children generally reflect their parents' standards of behavior. They would take us into the kitchen, which at the Shklovskis' was run like a cafeteria, give us food and drink, and entertain us with their chatter. Vasia, who played the viola, always told us about the latest concert – at that time Shostakovich's symphony was all the rage. Shklovski listened to what Vasia said and commented gleefully: "That puts Shostakovich right at the top!" Those were times in which everybody had to be given his precise place in the hierarchy . . . The State encouraged people to behave like the boyars in medieval Russia . . . It was in those days that Lebedev–Kumach, who was said to be actually a very modest man, found himself elevated to the status of "top poet." Shklovski also had his ambitions, but he wanted to see things decided on the basis of his famous "Hamburg reckoning." M. would have loved to go and hear Shostakovich's new symphony, but we were afraid to miss the last train.

With Varia the conversation was different. She showed us her school textbooks where the portraits of Party leaders had thick pieces of paper pasted over them as one by one they fell into disgrace – this the children had to do on instructions from their teacher. Varia said how much she would like to cover up Semashko – "We'll have to sooner or later, so why not now?" At this time the editors of encyclopedias and reference books were sending subscribers – most such works were bought on subscription – lists of articles that had to be pasted over or cut out. In the Shklovski household this was attended to by Victor himself. With every new arrest, people went through their books and burned the works of disgraced leaders in their stoves. In new apartment buildings, which had central heating instead of stoves, forbidden books, personal diaries, correspondence and other "subversive literature" had to be cut up in pieces with scissors and thrown down the toilet. People were kept very busy . . .

Nikita, the least talkative of the children sometimes said things that staggered the grown–ups. Once, for instance, Victor was telling us that he and Paustovski had been to see a famous bird fancier who trained canaries – he only had to give a sign for one of his birds to come out of its cage, sit on a perch and sing. On another signal from its owner, it obediently went back into its cage again. "Just like a member of the Union of Writers," said Nikita and left the room. After saying something like this, he always disappeared into his own room, where he kept the birds he had caught. But he treated his birds nicely, and didn't believe in training them. He told us that songbirds always learned to sing from certain older birds that were particularly good at it. In the Kursk region, once famous for its nightingales, the best songsters had all been caught, and young birds had no way of learning any more. The Kursk "school" of nightingales was thus destroyed because of the selfish people who had put the best songsters in cages.

When Vasilisa with her smiling light–blue eyes arrived, she at once went into action. She ran a bath for us and gave us underclothes. She would give me hers and M. Victor's; then she made us lie down for a rest. Victor was always trying to think of ways of helping M., apart from entertaining him with the latest gossip. In the late autumn he gave him an old coat made of dog skin which the previous winter had been worn by Andronikov, the "one-man orchestra." But since then Andronikov had come up in the world and had got himself a brand-new coat of the kind his status as a member of the Writers' Union entitled him to. Shklovski now solemnly handed the dog-skin coat over to M. and even made a little speech on the occasion: "Let everybody see that you came here riding inside the train, not hanging on the buffers . . ." Till then M. had worn a yellow coat made of leather – also a gift from somebody. It was in this yellow coat that he went to the camp later on.

Whenever the doorbell rang, they hid us in the kitchen or the children's room before opeining the door. If it was a friend, we were at once released from captivity with shouts of joy, but if it was Pavlenko or Lelia Povolotskaya, the woman police spy from next door – the one who had a stroke when they started rehabilitating people – we stayed in our hiding place until they were gone. None of them ever once caught a glimpse of us, and we were very proud of the fact.

The Shklovskis' house was the only place where we felt like human beings again. This was a family that knew how to help lost souls like us. In their kitchen we discussed our problems – where to stay the night, how to get money, and so forth. We avoided staying the night with them, because of the women who looked after the building – the janitress, the doorwoman and the one who worked the elevator. It was a time-honored tradition that these down-trodden but good-natured souls worked for the secret police. They got no extra pay for this – it simply counted as part of their normal duties. I don't remember now how we managed it, but we did go to the Shostakovich concert and stayed the night somewhere else . . .

When I later came by myself to the Shklovskis' apartment, after M.'s death, the women at the door asked me where he was, and when I told them he was dead, they sighed. "But we thought you'd be the first to go," said one of them. This remark showed me the extent to which our fate had been written on our faces, and it also made me realize that these wretched women had hearts after all, and that one needn't be so afraid of them. The ones who took pity on me soon died – the poor women didn't last long on their meager rations – but afterward I always got on well with their successors, who never informed the militia that I sometimes spent the night at the Shklovskis'. Returning home after midnight I always gave them twenty or thirty copecks, because they had to get up to unlock a door for me. Only after the monetary reform of 1961 did we realised that those tips were just miserable two or three copecks. That's how the word can hypnotise us. For instance, there still was some charm in the word "ruble," so we felt worse parting with five rubles before reform than parting with fifty copecks afterward. And it was considered quite generous to give a ruble to a taxi-driver as a tip, but not ten copecks now.

. . . But in 1937 we were terrified of being reported and tried not to stay at the Shklovskis' for fear of getting them into trouble — instead, we kept on the move all the time chasing breathlessly from place to place.

Occasionally, when there was no choice, we stayed the night there nevertheless, sleeping on their bedroom floor on a mattress covered with a sheepskin rug. They were on the seventh story, so you couldn't hear cars stopping outside, but if ever we heard the elevator coming up at night, we all four of us raced to the door and listened. "Thank God," we would say, "it's downstairs" or "it's gone past." This business of listening for the elevator happened every night, no matter whether we were there or not. Fortunately, it was not used all that often, since many of the writers with apartments in the building spent most of their time in Peredelkino, or in any case didn't come home late — and their children were still very young. In the years of the terror, there was not a home in the country where people did not sit trembling at night, their ears straining to catch the murmur of passing cars or the sound of the elevator. Even nowadays, whenever I spend the night at the Shklovskis' apartment, I tremble as I hear the elevator go past. The sight of half-dressed people huddling by the door, waiting to hear where the elevator stops, is something one can never forget.

One night recently, after a car had stopped outside my house, I had a bad dream in which I thought M. was waking me up and saying: "Get dressed — they've come for you this time." But I refused to budge: "I won't get up — to hell with them!" This was a mental revolt against what is also, after all, a kind of collaboration: they come to cart you off to prison and you just meekly get out of bed and put on your clothes with trembling hands. But never again! If they come for me, they'll have to carry me out on a stretcher or kill me on the spot — I'll never go of my own free will.

Once during the winter of 1937 we decided it was wrong to go on taking advantage of the Shklovskis' kindness. We were afraid of compromising them — a single denunciation and they could all land in prison. We were horrified at the thought of bringing disaster on Shklovski and his whole family, and though they begged us not to worry, we stopped going to see them for a while. As a result, we felt more homeless and lonely than ever before. Soon M. could stand it no longer and while we were on a visit to Lev Bruni he phoned the Shklovskis. "Come over at once," said Victor, "Vasilisa misses you terribly." A quarter of an hour later we rang at their door and Vasilisa came out crying tears of joy. I then felt that the only reality in the world was that woman's blue eyes. And I still think so.

*Translated by Max Hayward*

*Copyright © 1970 by Atheneum Publishers*

Ruth Zernova

# WHY NOW?

*For Katya Zvorykina*

When Leo Tolstoy died, Baba Lyuba was forty-seven years old and
had already been a widow for a long time. Her little girl, Nyurka,
who was growing up and nearly finished high school, watched
everything with black eyes that glittered as fiercely as her dead
father's. Her mother took an interest in her high school triumphs, but
also invited the rabbi over, so that Nyurka would not forget who she
was. One hot day Nyurka came home all upset and said that Leo
Tolstoy had died.

"Count Tolstoy?" sighed Baba Lyuba. She remembered that name
from her girlhood: hiding from her strict father the watchmaker, she
had read *Anna Karenina.* "How can this happen? Who is left?"

"Now, you have to admit, there are still a few writers alive," said
her daughter. "Kuprin, Leonid Andreyev, Maxim Gorky,
Artsybashev. But who were they, compared with Tolstoy?"

As if her mother were arguing with her. Such a well-read girl!
". . . he didn't even die at home. By the time you find out the details here in Yeniseysk, they've already buried him!"
"What do you have against Yeniseysk?" Her mother was offended.
"It's boring!" said Nyurka. "In Irkutsk at least there's some life. But here it's boring."
"Boring! At your age I didn't even know the word."
"Look at Leo Tolstoy. He got bored at home, and he left."
"And how old was he? Seventy, isn't that right?"
"Eighty-two!" said Nyurka triumphantly.
Baba Lyuba pursed her lips meaningfully and said, "Twelve years over the alloted span. That's good."
The alloted span, by her Jewish reckoning, was threescore years and ten.
And now she herself had long since gone beyond that span, and beyond Tolstoy's; and at first it made her anxious and afraid. But then she decided to make time stand still; and so for ten years now she'd been telling everyone that she's eighty-four.
Those years went by, sometimes slowly, sometimes quickly. Nyurka finished high school and right away she married a Jewish veterinarian, a serious young man, and now came the Revolution and now Zhorzhik was born, named in honor of Baba Lyuba's father – they somehow turned Hirsh into George, everybody does that now. Thanks be to God, at least they circumcised him! And now they went to Petersburg. Petersburg had also changed its name – to Petrograd, to Leningrad. And now Nyurka got divorced – not right away, but after a while; and as a matter of fact, that veterinarian – a stranger, after all – better off without him; and Nyurka started working – with retarded children, in a special home. For a while life went on quietly, slowly, at its own pace: Zhorzhik grew, a wonderful boy; always getting in fights, it's true – but after all, he was a boy. At home he'd fight with the little boys over the candy-wrappers they all collected; then at school he'd fight with them again over a certain Katya. He was constantly making up poems about this Katya; but Katya didn't fall in love with him. Thanks be to God: Baba Lyuba didn't like her. Different girls would come to the house – Zhorzhik liked some, Baba Lyuaba liked others – and Baba Lyuba would say, What do you do, hypnotize them, or what? Zhorzhik had the same

100

fiercely glittering eyes as Nyurka, but in a man that wasn't a bad thing. On the whole he was a high-spirited boy, but with a heart of gold.

And then, once again — bang! Zhorzhik graduated from the University, got married, and war broke out — all at once. And now they were all alone again, a widow and her daughter, as if the whole thing had been a dream. No Leningrad, no Yeniseysk, just Vyatka. Not Vyatka now, but Kirov (was Kirov born there, do you think?) — snowdrifts, wooden houses, the forest nearby. They managed; they didn't go hungry. Nyurka had a worker's ration because of the retarded children; and Zhorzhik had his officer's allotment sent to them instead of to his wife, because right away his wife took off, didn't even send letters, went back to her parents somewhere in the south. She was never heard from again. Zhorzhik returned from the war whole and unharmed, except that his arm wouldn't bend — well, he wasn't musician, thanks be to God, even with an arm like that he could still. . . And Milochka appeared in their house, and Baba Lyuba fell in love with her — not right away, of course, but after a while. What pleased her most was that Milochka was a blonde.

"I want for my grandchildren to be blonde," said Baba Lyuba.

"Where would you put grandchildren, Baba Lyuba! With four of us in one room, as it is," said Mila.

"Not counting the maid," remarked Nyurka, who was called Anna Abramovna now.

"And the television," added Zhorzhik.

Baba Lyuba had fallen in love with the television set and would not allow it to be turned off. So her granddaughter, Verka, grew up in front of a television set. Baba Lyuba was secretly glad that it was a granddaughter and not a grandson: whenever she'd tried to talk to Zhorzhik about circumcision he'd made fun of her. Finally Nyurka had told her that he could get in trouble at work. That they were very strict now about circumcision. And during the war Zhorzhik had joined the Party. But thanks be to God, the baby was a girl — Verka, a wonderful little girl, and smart; and no fights, no unpleasantness, in all those ten years.

Now everyone is saying: changes, changes! Baba Lyuba didn't like changes, they just meant trouble. What further changes could

101

there be? Stalin died, and thanks be to God, and there haven't been any real changes, only talk, and life goes on quietly, at its own pace, slowly, thanks be to God! Nyurka has retired, the children go to work, Verka goes to school.

Verka hadn't turned out to be blonde — she had dark hair and very black eyes with a fierce sparkle. "Just like her dead father's," said Baba Lyuba with displeasure, not quite knowing whether the father she meant was hers or her daughter's. "He'd look at me, and my soul would sink to my shoes!" "Grandma, Zhorzhik has the same eyes, and you're not afraid." "Zhorzhik! Zhorzhik, a hypnotist! He hypnotizes everybody. He even hypnotized you. What's the matter with you, couldn't you find anyone to marry? And you such a beauty!"

Mila laughed. She'd only been called a beauty once in her life, during the evacuation.

And look how much time had passed, and she remembered everything.

Into the washroom of the Institute dormitory, where Mila was washing clothes under the faucet, had come a short, skinny officer in a tunic unbelted over army breeches, wearing small slippers made for a woman's feet. Everybody was reading *War and Peace* then, and Mila thought, "A modern Prince Bolkonsky!"

Prince Bolkonsky took off his tunic, poured cold water over himself down to his waist, then started washing his legs right under the spigot. Mila stole a look at him. He looked at her too, seemed surprised at something, looked again, put on his tunic and said without moving any closer, "You know what, the way things are now, nobody will tell you. The war — people don't know how to behave any more, they've gotten hard. So *I'll* tell you. You're beautiful. You're a beauty, and you don't know it, because there's nobody to tell you. But, please, remember that I told you."

He turned and went out, and maybe he went away that very day — to the front or the rear, wherever he had to go. Mila never saw him again. And no one ever again told her she was a beauty — only Baba Lyuba. And she did it more out of gratitude for a happy relationship, for the fact that she had married Zhorzhik and lived with them in one room, all five, and of course, for the fact that she was blonde. Already Mila was helping Nature and coloring with henna the grey roots of her long, wild hair; already its hue was getting strange, sort of red. Baba Lyuba marvelled the whole time: so blonde, such a beauty. He hypnotized you!

"Mama!" interrupted Anna Abramovna. "Why open Milochka's eyes? What if she leaves Zhorzhik?"

Baba Lyuba waved her away and said to Mila,

"Don't pay any!"

"Don't pay any!" was a family legacy from a long-ago pupil of Anna Abramovna's, a retarded child called Val'ka. Val'ka had a kind heart. When Anna Abramovna cried over her pranks — she'd thrown an inkwell at the social science teacher, she'd spent the night in the boys' dormitory — Val'ka would come up to her, pat her on the shoulder, and say,

"Forget it, don't pay any! Am I worth getting upset over? Don't pay any!"

Once, on account of this Val'ka, Anna Abramovna's teaching career was almost cut short. And not just her career: she herself could easily have disappeared for a good ten years, or forever. There was an incident during the thirties, at the morning school assembly, in front of the Committee. Val'ka came up onto the platform and began to read a poem about the building of socialism -- it might have been one that Zhorzhik had written as a child.

> The Party made a bargain:
> To cultivate its garden

Familiar rhymes suddenly clicked in her head. For some reason she glanced around, then looked into the audience, at the Committee, and gleefully concluded:

> And now they beg your pardon,
> Each sadly naked bush!

She stuck her tongue out at the Committee, burst out laughing, and ran off into the wings, where they were already calming Anna Abramovna down with valerian drops. But it all blew over. Either the Committee hadn't noticed, or Val'ka's protruding tongue had muffled everything. But after that Anna Abramovna had more frequent bad spells with her heart. After every bad spell, Baba Lyuba would lament,

"She takes after her father. On my side of the family, nobody even knew they *had* a heart."

Every summer they went to a *dacha* on the Karelian isthmus; they rented a room with a veranda. When Zhorzhik came on Saturday, he and Mila slept on the veranda, even when the radio forecast called for "early autumn frost on the ground." After these nights with her husband, Mila would invariably come down with a cold. She'd move into the common room. There the usual warm crowdedness reigned: the treadle sewing machine (a Singer), Baba Lyuba's armchair, the television, Verka's toybox, Mila's professional books — a hundred and fifty kilograms' worth. Verka's friends would come over, the neighbors' sons. Baba Lyuba would squint at them suspiciously.

When Mila appeared in the doorway, Baba Lyuba would whisper, "They're truying to lure Maruska away."

Ten years before, when Verka was born, a maid named Maruska had taken care of her. After that, though the maids changed frequently, Baba Lyuba couldn't be bothered learning new names. But by some strange coincedence, the latest maid, a Finnish girl, was called Marya Adamovna.

"Grandma! What are you talking about? They're just children."

"They're trying to get her away from us. Watch how they wink at her."

"Grandma, you're getting crochety."

"What of it," answered Baba Lyuba proudly. "At my age, I'm entitled. Thanks be to God — eighty-four years old."

But sometimes Baba Lyuba took offense. Or it just felt suffocating in the room at the dacha, filled with city furniture. And out she'd go, without a word to anyone.

Anna Abramovna would come up to Mila, sitting among her manuscripts. She'd raise her head. Anna Abramovna would roll her eyes and snort.

"Again?" Mila would ask.

"Again."

"Oh, Lord!"

Mila would push her books aside and get heavily to her feet.

"That woman will drive me out of my mind! I know what I'll do. I'll write a screenplay — *Old Women Should Know Their Place.*"

"My place is by the kerosene heater," answered Anna Abramovna.

"Fine," said Mila. "I'll go out along the road by myself."

And she went out. The road was dusty. Along came Verka riding her bicycle, with the neighbors' sons.

"Vera!" Mila shouted. "Ride to the corner, see if she's there."

"Again?" Verka asked. And she explained to the boys, "Baba Lyuba went off again, like Leo Tolstoy."

The bicycles were carried off in a whirlwind of dust, with Mila walking quickly after them. Then the riders came flying back around the bend, straight at her.

"Aunt Mila!" shouted the boys. "There, on the corner of Konnaya Street!"

"She's standing there," reported Vera, braking close to her mother. "Looking off into the distance."

Mila went up to Baba Lyuba. "Grandma!" she breathed. "Why didn't you tell anybody. . . ."

Baba Lyuba smiled sweetly. "I just felt like it," she said in an insincere voice. "I got the urge to take a walk, breathe a little air."

"But this is a main road, there are cars. They'll hit you, and then what? What's the matter with you, don't you understand?"

"Why wouldn't I understand?" Baba Lyuba was offended. "What am I, a cow?"

She threaded her limp, wasted hand peaceably through the crook of Mila's arm and said,

"Let's go home. We've had our walk, and that's enough."

"Grandma," said Mila. "I have to have your guarantee that you won't go out any more without asking."

"I won't give you any more guarantees," answered Baba Lyuba angrily. "I've already given you a guarantee."

"But that was about dishes."

"What's the difference?" Baba Lyuba was angry. "A guarantee is a guarantee."

The guarantee concerning dishes, written in Mila's hand, said: *I solemnly promise never again to wash dishes, not in hot, nor in cold, nor in river, nor in sea, nor in well water.*

Baba Lyuba had read it and said,

"And have you forgotten rain water? You lawyer!"

"You should also say, Javelle water," Mila had added.

"What did you say? Javelle?"

And she had written down, *nor rain, nor Javelle.* Signed: *Lyuba Shapiro.*

Shapiro was Baba Lyuba's maiden name.

And every summer the whole thing would be repeated. Both the guarantees and the excursions. But this past summer the excursions came more often, and what was worse, Baba Lyuba would refuse to come back.

"I'll wait for Zhorzhik, then I'll come home," she'd announce. "I won't come till then."

"Grandma! But he's not supposed to come today. Today isn't Friday."

"But last Friday he didn't come. Can you deny that?"

Mila couldn't object. The fact was, he hadn't.

"You and Nyurka think Grandma's gotten senile. Well, now you see — she hasn't! I'll *spot you one* on that." Baba Lyuba remembered this expression from Zhorzhik's childhood. "Where is he running around, who with? What is it, has he fallen into bad company?"

And, confusing family relations again,

"You're his mother, you should know! But you don't take any interest at all. You just want to read your books. *Nov-els!*"

She screwed up her face and stuck out her lower lip to express her disdain for novels. Mila answered cheerfully,

"I don't *read* them, Grandma. I write about them."

"What are we having for dinner?" asked Baba Lyuba eagerly. "Fritters again?"

"Apple fritters. Apple fritters, Grandma."

And Baba Lyuba gave in. Maybe because of tradition. It was a family saying that Baba Lyuba couldn't hold out against fritters. And she kept up her legend, her myth, because she felt her position demanded it; no doubt Don Juan felt the same way about his one-thousand-third Spanish Lady.


Zhorzhik, to everyone's delight, came after all — not on Friday but on Saturday, and stayed on Sunday. They hadn't been expecting him. He stayed, complaining about everything: lunch, the weather, Verka's staying home, Grandma's peregrinations.

"Like the very wrath of God!" said Anna Abramovna, rolling her eyes, and she snorted and elbowed Mila.

"I'm a meat-and-potatoes man!" announced Zhorzhik. "It's a fact of my poetic biography. Without potatoes, dinner isn't dinner for me, not if you give me ten cutlets."

"I'll go to the Shermans', maybe they've got some potatoes," said his mother.

"Too late," said her son gloomily. "I'll go myself, maybe Lyova has come."

He played chess with the Shermans' Lyova. But Lyova wasn't there. He came back in no time and started in on Verka.

"Why don't you go out and play? Why aren't you out riding with the other children?"

Vera's face fell. She said,

"They aren't friends with me now. They're friends with fat Lena. Because she has something I don't."

"What does she have?" asked Zhorzhik curiously. His mother sent him a warning glance and he bit his tongue. But Vera, already crying, said,

"Arsik!"

And she began to sob. Anna Abramovna put her arms around her and explained to Zhorzhik that Arsik was a poodle.

"Ah!" said Zhorzhik.

He switched to his grandmother.

"Grandma! What's this they tell me? Why do you go out walking on the road? In an old-fashioned, worn-out *shushun?*"

"Why would I have a fashionable one?" objected Baba Lyuba. "Thanks be to God, eighty-four years old."

"And the cars?"

"And what about the cars? Suppose a car hits me — who will cry for me?"

"I'll cry for you, Grandma," said Zhorzhik, his eyes flashing wildly. "You give me your solem promise that you won't. . . ."

Baba Lyuba was beginning to thaw, but she answered angrily,

"Don't you hypnotize me! Don't look at me like that!"

"I'm looking at you with love! Well? Do you promise?"

"I promise, I promise!"

Waiting for supper, Zhorzhik began to pace the veranda and mutter to himself under his breath. "'We children of Russia's terrible years'," he muttered, "'Nothing, nothing, can we forget'." Suddenly he came to a stop.

"But them? Children of Russia's terrible years?" he cried. "What terrible things have *they* seen? The Russo-Japanese war? The Steregushchiy Memorial?"

"They kept waiting for them to happen," said Mila, raising her head from her book. "There's terror in waiting, too. Remember the winter of fifty-three?"

Zhorzhik bent his head, thought for a minute, then nodded.

"You smart little bunny," he said, and pinched Mila on the cheek. She blushed, as much as her weathered skin allowed.

In the middle of July the weather turned into real autumn. Cold rain fell in heavy sheets.

"We're always swimming against the current," sighed Anna Abramovna. "Everybody else goes south. Leningraders go north, to the Karelian isthmus."

She had never been south. Her veterinarian husband had promised during their first year of married life that he would transfer to a job in Yalta and she'd come there in the summer with their son. He kept his promise — he transferred. The first summer, Anna Abramovna couldn't go — she was still taking courses — and the next summer he didn't send for her. "And not for any particular reason," she recounted afterwards, "just becouse he was a lone wolf. A lone wolf by nature. For the next ten years he lived alone. He sent money regularly for Zhorzhik's support. That's how we lived — me here, him there. Then he got it into his head to get married."

Anna Abramovna snorted.

Marya Adamovna loved this story. She would sit there darning Verka's stockings and say,

"Well, come on, Anna Abramovna, tell us about how you and your husband used to live. Him in Yalta, you in Leningrad."

"What's there to tell?"

But Anna Abramovna would tell the story, and Marya Adamovna would listen to her intently and then say,

"Well, good thing you didn't move there. Even in Gatchina there's nothing; only fifty kilometers away, and they have to bring everything from Leningrad! Even fruits and vegetables, even housewares. And where does he end up — in Yalta. A place you can only get to by boat."

Anna Abramovna would become thoughtful.

"And now I'll tell you about my farmer," Marya Adamovna would say. "Have I told you about the Estonian I worked for? The one who lives next-door to my sister?"

"Tell me," Anna Abramovna would say diplomatically. She knew the story by heart.

109

". . . and they stick him in prison as a partisan, for ten years. And him a bee-farmer."

"Beekeeper," says Baba Lyuba from her chair.

"Whatever. So Baba Lyuba's listening. Well, and so last year they let him out. That German, the head guy who replaced Hitler – after he got in."

"Adenauer," says Mila without raising her head from her book.

". . . And his whole place had been torn up, naturally, the beehives empty, only the posts standing. He came home in the morning, and in the evening! . . In the evening a swarm flew in. Well, he was just out of his mind with joy. He came running to my sister, weeping out loud. And my sister is such a practical person! He says, 'Think of it,' he says, 'Marusya, just this morning I arrived, and in the evening they flew back to me!' And he keeps talking and crying, and talking and crying . . ."

"Baba Anya!" begs Vera. "It looks like the rain has stopped. Can I ride my bike?"

"The weather is willy-nilly," Marya Adamovna points out.

And Vera comes to the conclusion that they'll never let her go outside again.

"And Zhorzhik won't come, again," Baba Lyuba muttered. "In this weather, what is he, crazy – go to a *dacha?* What is he, never seen an old woman? There are old women in the city."

"And young ones, too," says Vera thoughtfully, without having anything in mind; and she wonders why everyone bursts out laughing.

"I've never understood the reasons for my son's success," says Anna Abramovna insincerely. "They call up, they don't say anything, just breathe heavily into the receiver. What is it about him that attracts them? Short, with an arm that won't bend . . ."

"And a crooked nose!" Marya Adamovna joins in. "But women are fools. What do they know? A man's not a creep, they think he's handsome."

"He hypnotizes them," says Mila, not at all depressed by

110

talk of her husband's successes. "Baba Lyuba knows."

"And did he hypnotize you?"

"Me, he read his poetry. And I'll tell you right now, he's a real poet."

Mila loved poetry, and she forgave her husband a lot because he was a poet, even though he wore out the seat of his pants at his scientific institute. She had her own ideas about the poetic metabolism. A girlhood friend had said to her,

"You give him an awful lot of freedom!"

Mila had smiled. She and her friend had had different destinies. In her youth her friend suffered from what Alexey Almazov called a "pathological hypertrophy of the sexual element." She was fourteen when her stepfather seduced her; at fifteen, she had her first abortion; at twenty, she was a woman with a past. At tweny-five or so, she broke with the past and married someone with a future. Now she and her husband had their own *dacha* not far from the one Mila and her family rented.

"Never mind, Vera," Marya Adamovna comforted, "tomorrow will be good weather, papa will come, you'll have plenty of time to ride your bike."

But the weather didn't get better, and no one came, and the bicycle stood unused, and Mila felt sort of . . . Baba Lyuba said, "Our Mila is pregnant. It's time to go back to the city."

"Mama, what are you talking about!" Anna Abramovna was shocked. "Pregnant! How? She's forty years old."

"Baba Lyuba always says that Mila's pregnant," said Marya Adamovna. "Even that winter, remember, when there was flu all over."

This time, however, Baba Lyuba turned out to be right. In August Mila still had doubts. But when they moved back to the city (sewing machine, Baba Lyuba's armchair, Vera's bed, Vera's toybox, the television set, books – Mila helped load everything), there was no longer any doubt. She had to make a decision. And in the evenings, while Marya Adamovna snored and Baba Lyuba dozed in her chair, Mila would consult Anna Abramovna. Anna Abramovna rolled eyes — Where can we put another bed, do you suppose? — then snorted cheerfully. At that unlikley moment, Baba Lyuba announced loudly,

"I hear everything, you can't keep secrets from me! Just think, a miracle — she's pregnant. Not a virgin, thanks be to God!"

"Who's pregnant?" Verka woke up.

Marya Adamovna woke up and grumbled, "Go to sleep, Vera, go to sleep. What kind of talk is that for a little girl? 'Pregnant, pregnant!' Go to sleep!"

"Everybody yells at me," muttered Vera, falling asleep,

And where was Zhorzhik? Why, Zhorzhik had gotten in into his head to get married. At the Registry. He and Mila weren't registered: he had somehow forgotten to dissolve his pre-war marriage. Mila didn't even think of thinking about it, what with her job, Verka, intrigues at work. She was constantly afraid they would dismiss her for being a Jew, and so she fulfilled the Plan for her whole department. Her position at work, right up until 'fifty-six, seemed to her temporary and somehow illegal. Even in that room with Zhorzhik, Anna Abramovna, Baba Lyuba, Verka, and Marya Adamovna, she lived illegally — without a *propiska*. Her *propiska* was for the apartment where she was born, and there, in what was officially her room, lived almost total strangers — her sister's former husband and his new wife. Anna Abramovna would sometimes say that they ought to exchange their two rooms for two together. Mila would joke, when Vera is ready to get married — then we'll do it. She had grown used to this warm crowdedness. Sometimes Anna Abramovna would come into the kitchen and roll her eyes.

"I think Machamolets has been hinting about papers."

Machamolets — the Angel of Death — was what she called gloomy Ivan Fyodorovich, the tenant in charge of their apartment.

But the whole business went no further than hints. The hinting had always been connected with the fact that Mila took too long in the common bathroom. Mila began going to the public baths, and the hints stopped. And that was how she lived, without a *propiska.*

Well, so Zhorzhik got into his head to get married. Not Mila, however. The news came from the place where he worked. A jealous female voice phoned. "Is this Anna Abramovna?"

"Yes," said Anna Abramovna.

"Do you know that your son is planning to register his marriage to Marina Fedotovna Ivanova?"

"What do you mean?" asked Anna Abramovna, without thinking (afterward she could never forgive herself).

"They're having an affair," said the voice. "We've known for a long time, but now . . . We think the family ought to know."

Anna Abramovna was silent for a little while, collecting her thoughts; then she asked, "And who is 'we'?"

"We're his coworkers."

"And what's *your* name? Is it Tamara?"

"It's not important," said the voice, faltering.

"No. Why 'not important'? Are you in the habit of breathing heavily into the receiver?"

The receiver gave a heavy breath and went silent. Anna Abramovna sat down in a chair and started to cry. Baba Lyuba dozed. There was no one else at home. Anna Abramovna decided to speak to her son.

But where? When Zhorzhik and Mila needed to have things out, they usually went to the movies. But he hadn't gone to the movies with his mother for many years. She had to wait for an opportunity; but the opportunity never came. He came home late, ate his meat and potatoes, and fell into bed.

*"Forty Years on a Folding Cot* – a title for my memoirs," he would grumble.

In the morning he and Vera rushed out together. Then Marya Adamovna cleared the table, Mila spread out her manuscripts, Anna Abramovna sat down at the sewing machine, baba Lyuba turned on the television.

"Mila!" she'd ask. "What river is that? The Yenisey?"

"No, Grandma, the Neva," Mila would answer, without raising her head.

Baba Lyuba would shrug her shoulders, skeptical.

"Why now?"

Marya Adamovna came into the kitchen and announced, "If you won't buy a separate electric meter, I won't live with you. That, that — Machamolka — is saying we use too much electricity again. I know it isn't us, but how can you prove it? Two of you working, and you can't manage to get a meter!"

"Okay, Marya Adamovna," said Mila cheerfully. "Let's really splurge. We'll buy ourselves a meter."

"And a washboard," said Marya Adamovna.

"And a washboard. No, wait — we won't buy a washboard. We'll buy a table lamp."

After arguing some more, Marya Adamovna went out. In a little while Mila raised her head and said,

"How are we going to decide, Anna Abramovna? Time is running out. This can't wait."

And at once Anna Abramovna decided. "Mila, I think you should talk to Zhorzhik."

At any other time, Mila would have answered, But why? He'll just say, Bunny, do what you think best. But it was so painful for Anna Abramovna to speak, that Mila subconsciously caught a signal she pricked up her ears.

"What is it?"

Stumbling over her words, wiping her eyes every other minute and sniffing, Anna Abramovna told about the telephone call. Mila's face grew darker. She was silent, then she said exasperatedly,

"What a fool! He has to pick *now!*"

She wanted to keep the baby. She felt well, looked well, didn't even know the phrase "morning sickness"; just the opposite — she wanted to eat all the time, everything tasted good. Verka — she could no longer pick her up or cuddle her, really; and her relations with her husband had never made her happy as far as the intimate side went, even though it was because of that side that she had shivered patiently on the veranda of the *dacha*. She endured it as a shameful and joyless but inescapable part of family life. But in the city! The hasty muzzle-nuzzling in the night, with everyone feigning sleep; the measured creaking of the bed, the terrible din of breathing — could the dead sleep through it? — she just prayed, Hurry up, hurry up! Fortunately, in the city it happened seldom.

What could you do, if that was the only way to have children. She would like to keep the baby. Yes, but remember Verka. The first month she never slept, and she and Zhorzhik had taken turns carrying her in their arms — one sleeping, the other walking her.

"No, it's awful, awful, how could I, alone — and while he's — No, it's awful, awful, how can I keep it?" And she remembered the Friend, with whom even now she still had conversations about love. Mila had always maintained that in love you were free as a bird; the Friend insisted love was chains. Now she would say, "You *see*!" Or look at her with compassion. Mila pushed aside the damned manuscripts and began to pace — three steps over, three steps back. "I'm an old fool," she muttered. "Damn, damn, damn."

"Mila," Baba Lyuba asked drowsily, "do you remember Old Grisha's last name?"

"I don't remember, Grandma."

"What Old Grisha?" asked Anna Abramovna.

"The one they cursed in synagogue. Well? The one who, aftewards, he fell through a hole in the ice. Well? Why are you pretending you don't remember?"

"Now I remember," said Anna Abramovna. "The one who converted and went off to the gold fields?"

"Well? And his last name?"

"I don't remember his last name. Let me think."

"Think, think. Just don't fall asleep. The Devil knows what your head is filled with."

And she started to doze off.

But it wasn't easy to fall asleep. Clouds hung in the room, right over her head, and she had to run home as fast as she could before the storm, and she had to save someone as fast as she could, someone next to her, someone very small. And they hurry but it's hard to hurry, not enough breath, but there's no rain yet, just the clouds hanging low.

They woke her, put a plate of soup on the table in front of her. She was angry.

"What's this soup doing here? Tea with raspberry jam — that's what I need. Otherwise, the storm . . ."

Then she realized that there was no storm, they must have managed to outrun it, only why were thay all here, these people with wild eyes — Nyurka, Verka, but not the one she needed.

"Mila," she kept asking sadly, "he still hasn't come?"

And remembered who he was: her son. No, her grandson. Oh, never mind. Zhorzhik.

At one point Mila answered furiously, "He'll come. When it's feeding time, he'll come!"

Baba Lyuba actually tried to raise herself up a little — Mila's voice was strange. She collected her thoughts and pronounced,

"A good Jewish woman, and she sounds like a Siberian hag."

She became suspicious of Mila. It was from her that the clouds came which hung from the ceiling. It was from her that the little one had to be saved. When Mila put a glass of tea in front of her, she said inaudibly,

"From your hands, I won't take!"

Mila burst into tears, began to laugh, cried out in her former cheerful voice,

"Grandma, if you turn against me, I don't know what I'll do!"

Baba Lyuba didn't believe the cheerful voice and went on looking at Mila suspiciously. Then she fell asleep. The tea got cold. Loud conversation woke her. Mila was saying,

"You should have told me sooner. Now it's too late for an abortion. Four months."

What abortion? thought Baba Lyuba. She already has a child.

Then his voice rang out.

"I will not abdicate my paternal re-spon-si-bil-i-ties!"

"Zhorzhik!" she called out.

"Coming, Mama. Coming. Look, you could at least think of her."

What are they all talking about, thought Baba Lyuba. Some foolishness. Why are they all angry with him? Look, they're yelling again.

Anna Abramovna was speaking with strained calmness.

"Whatever happens, your duty right now is to give your child a name. Just register with Milochka and then get a divorce and marry, don't marry, it's all the same. You don't want your child to have a blank on its birth certificate? You adopted Verka; but this one? She won't let you."

*A blank, a blank,* Baba Lyuba heard in her sleep. For some reason, sleep came over her now, when she didn't expect it and hadn't asked for it, right in the middle of the day, when they were talking foolishness. But at night when everyone is asleep, she wakes and imagines – God knows what: it can't be, what she imagines. They are weeping, they are mourning him. But he's alive; is it possible to mourn the living?

"Why are you mourning him?" she asked angrily. "How can you mourn the living?"

"What are you talking about, Mama," said Anna Abramovna, quickly wiping her eyes.

"You know what he's like. It's always the same story with him. Remember how he used to run away from home, back when we lived on Zelenin Street."

"I remember," Baba Lyuba began to nod. "But we found him then. I brought him home from the *Politsia* myself."

"Yes, but it wasn't you, it was me. And it wasn't the *Politsia,* it was the *Militsia.* Well . . ."

"What's the difference! You just like to argue. So he's done it again?"

"Oh, Mama! Don't ask!"

So that's how it is. Don't ask. That means the worst.

Baba Lyuba turned toward the wall. Sleep came again, but a poor sleep, without hope or comfort, without attempts

117

to save or be saved. In her sleep she breathed heavily. Marya Adamovna listened to her a while and said,

"Soon she'll be out of her misery. She'll have to be. What's holding her together, except that she doesn'd want to die. Listen, I have a sister — I mean, what a practical woman! Stands in the doorway; hollers, 'Out of my house!' He scooted right out, and what do you think? She finally saw the light. Now she has the best dresses, the best coats, everything she earns goes on her back. And before? 'Ach, trousers for Senichka! Ach, something for Senichka for Red Army Day!' It was disgusting to see."

"Mama," said Vera. "Listen, maybe this time you'll understand. Here's the problem. A train starts out at point A . . ."

"From the day I was born I never understood problems with trains."

Vera sighed and said, "Papa knew how to solve them." Without noticing, she had begun to speak of him in the past tense.

"Mila," said Anna Abramovna very quietly. "Today I telephoned that Marina Fedotovna."

Mila threw up her hands.

"Lord! That's all I needed! Am I in a kindergarten, or what? What did you talk about, I'd be interested to know."

"Why are you being like that, Milochka? I — forgive me if I — I too — I'm not a stranger, after all, I too —"

"Anna Abramovna, dear." Mila jumped to her feet. "Don't pay any."

"That's just what I mean! You're just like Val'ka. 'Come on, don't pay any!'"

"God knows, Anna Abramovna, that's how it is in our situation. That's the main thing — Don't pay any. So then what?"

"I told her that Zhorzhik has to register with you, that there's going to be a baby. She said" — lightning flashed from Anna Abramovna's eyes — "she said, We'll see that the children are taken care of."

"All the same, I understand why Zhorzhik left her," Anna Abramovna said later to the Friend, who was trying to console her. "There's no tenderness in her. I waited, just sat and waited, for her to throw herself on me and weep. But the blood left her face, and that was all. No, she doesn't know how. She's silent, silent. Paces up and down between the table and the closet; gets grouchy; and that's it. The next day she's making jokes."

"And you?"

"I joke, too. What else is there to do? I don't even know if she ever loved him."

The Friend asked her, "Mila, did you love him at all?"

"The Devil only knows! Love, hate — it's all nonsense. Here's what I think: the baby will come, and I won't get any sleep, I won't have any help. So I seethe. And yet — love, hate — that's an entirely different matter. He's out of his mind; what can I do?"

"There's been talk at work, did you know? He was reprimanded by the Party."

"But he doesn't give a damn. This reprimand — you know what it's really about? Who started the whole thing? The 'Other Woman' was mad, the one he was fooling around with before. That Tamara. She was in the habit of phoning here and breathing into the receiver. Anna Abramovna and I were used to it, only we didn't know her name until he said to us, Oh, that must be Tamara. And she started the whole uproar. Now I know what's going on. I hear absolutely everything."

"Oh, you!" said the Friend. "The mind of a lion, and the heart of a chicken! Why don't you write the Party Organization yourself? Why does some Tamara have to do it?"

Mila pursed her lips in disgust.

"Listen, you sit there making faces, and you'll end up with an illegitimate child. But the Party Organization would see that he did it. You and your idiotic sentimentality. This isn't Stalin's day, no one will kick him out for immorality. But they'll help you."

Mila shrugged her shoulders. Mind of a lion, heart of a chicken. Maybe so. Last year, when a rehabilitated Jewish coworker had appeared at their Institute after a seven-year absence, she had asked him not to sit beside her at meetings, so they wouldn't think. . . . Afterwards Zhorzhik nearly tore her apart. But all the time he himself was saying over and over, You be more careful. At that time no one was sure of anything yet. But why drag the Party Organization into it?

Zhorzhik stopped coming home altogether; Mila wept at night, lying on her back so that the tears wouldn't stain the pillowcase.

Mila turned forty. That morning, combing her hair in front of the wardrobe, she looked at herself with love and pity. Yes, she had been beautiful: that man had been right. Her features, though they'd hardened, were still regular. Her ears small, close to her head. And her hair! Naturally, her complexion; and her figure too. . . . But even then it hadn't been much of a figure; just slender. Yes, she'd been beautiful, and it was all gone, and here she was forty, her years of being a sexy woman were over, and what had they gone on? Stupid to worry about being sexy — what mattered was having children. And here she'll have two children — and won't she take care of them, they appriciate her now at work; she is, without false modesty, a highly skilled specialist — you could say, as highly skilled as they come — now everyone realizes that and they're not going to let her go, those days are over. But let him pay, anyway. It's for the children's good, and for his, too. Mila knew very well what was good for him, and what was bad.

"Mila," Baba Lyuba called from her bed.

Mila went over to her.

"You tell me the truth", Baba Lyuba whispered, fastening a wasted hand on Mila's skirt. "Nyurka certainly won't. Tell me, was he baptized?"

Mila opened her mouth, but she couldn't speak. Lord, what strange forms old people's apprehensions took.

"You won't answer. He must have been baptized. I knew it."

"Grandma, what are you talking about? He would never. What's the matter with you, Grandma?"

Baba Lyuba wasn't listening to her. She was talking to

herself. "And when he was courting that − that high school girl, I knew even then it would lead to no good. Now they'll curse him in synagogue. But soon I'll be with God. I'll tell Him everything."

"Grandma, what are you talking about?"

"I'll tell Him everything. He took away my father, took away my husband. Nyurka's, too. How can we manage, women without men? What could we do? I'll explain the whole thing to Him, to God."

God was in full-dress uniform with glittering buttons, like the director of the *gymnasium* in Yeniseysk. If you don't start crying right away, if you explain everything calmly, He might even understand. She explained to Him, she explained and she took all the blame − she hadn't known how to raise him, and she didn't deserve to have any special fuss made over her in Heaven. She began to sing for God the old lullaby, *"Sei a frumer ind a guter"* (Be pilus and good) − and then when your mother of a Tsadik − Here comes the mother of a *Pravednik*, a Righteous One. But of course everyone knew this song, and God did too, naturally; and she really couldn't tell whether she'd convinced Him or not, because God went and in came her grandson and embraced her.

"Grandma!" he said merrily. "What are you doing here, Grandma?"

And then Baba Lyuba understood that she had already gone to God, that He had let her come back just for a moment to say goodbye to her grandson and tell him something very important. But what was the very important something? She didn't want to remember what the boy had done that was so awful, because once it's done you can't change anything, and that wasn't what God had let her come back for. She put her trembling arms around her grandson's thick, manly neck and, weeping with pity, she said,

"I forgive you. You know that, I forgive you."

Then she fell asleep, weeping, on Zhorzhik's shoulder; he laid her head carefully on the pillows. No one noticed when she stopped breathing. Anna Abramovna was saying that it would be bad for the child to have a blank; Zhorzhik was breaking the news that he would have to vacate the apartment because he and Marina Fyodotovna were planning to move into a co-op, but he understood, and he would wangle permission for a co-op for all of them too. Mila wondered where he'd get the money, and he said, "We'll find it!'; she snorted and said it was worth getting divorced just for that; and Anna Abramovna burst into tears. And then Marya Adamovna came into the room holding a saucepan, went up to the old woman's bed, exclaimed and cried out loudly,

"Be quiet, you chatterboxes! Baba Lyuba is dead."

And the new baby — it was a boy, fair and blue-eyed — was born, and in the new co-op, as a matter of fact: Zhorzhik proved himself a marvel of efficiency and hypnotized everybody. Everything he tried succeeded. Exept for one thing. He asked for the baby to be named Lyova, in honor of Baba Lyuba and Leo Tolstoy.

But Mila wouldn't agree. And she named the little boy Fyodor, in honor of Dostoyevsky.

*Translated by Ann Harleman*

Lidiia Chukovskaia

# MEMORIES OF ANNA AKHMATOVA

*January 1, 1962, Leningrad*

Wandering across the wasteland through the hospital corps, or
more accurately, the hospital wings, I, endlessly and fruitlessly,
search for "Therapy 4." Here, in the hospital in Gavan, after
another heart attack, lies Anna Andreevna. I'm moving along
sideways, guarding my face against the blizzard, turning and
weaving off my path. Yes, well, there's not really any path, not
even a trace of one, in the snow. Wasteland, corps, blizzard.
Nobody but nobody: everyone's probably sleeping off the
"get-together." I run into little signs, but never the right one:
"Surgery," "Urology," but the wasteland — empty. I would have
gone into "Surgery" and asked the coat check woman where's
"Therapy 4?" and would have gotten barked at: "What are ya'
blind? Or illiterate? Sur-ger-y." And I wasn't about to go
poking around in "Urinology." Snowstorm, wasteland. A few times
I come up to the doors of some building that has nothing written
on it; behind one set of the peeling swinging doors there seems to
be a storehouse: either a heap of rotten cabbage or scrapmetal.
Medicine obviously couldn't dwell behind doors like this. I move
back: same blizzard, cold, wasteland, same little signs "Surgery"
and "Urology" — and finally, in desperation, I shove the peeling
deathly-still door. There's damp dimness; but in the dark there's a
strip of light; I go on — another pair of doors — beyond them,
light and warmth, and you can take off your wet kerchief, brush
off your hat, coat, boots — even a little besom ready to use. A
friendly clock-room attendant took my things, not grumbling about
their being wet, gave me a bleached out but clean robe and told
me where to go.

Steep stairs, but clean.

Second floor. Here's the sign: "Therapy." And an unexpected
happy smell: Christmas, spruce. Big, old-fashioned hall, chairs
against the wall, and in the corner an honest to God Christmas
tree — full and tall as the ceiling.

123

Corridor. The first ward is on the left hand side. Here, in the corridor, there's already only the smell of old bedclothes and medicine. Hospital smells.

I'm on the threshold of the ward. The stuffiness is squeezing my heart. One window, four beds, crowded, quiet and stuffy, stuffy. Barely any room between the beds. Anna Andreevna is lying in the first bed to the right of the door. When I looked from the threshold – her face on the pillow was bitter, almost as though she had turned away from something, hurt. I hesitated: sleeping? Go or wait? But she herself immediately opened her eyes, saw me, cheered up and promptly sat up. Very much cheered, she said amiably,

"Well, now that you're here, I can believe that it's really the New Year."

And so began her monologue. She didn't ask me any questions, but spoke incessantly. Missed having an audience. It was her third heart attack. Now she's better, and they'll release her soon. Has a room at Komaróvo Writers Sanatorium from January 11, but she isn't sure she'll have strength enough to go. At home, thank God, they installed a phone because the doctor said he doesn't dare release one so sick to an apartment without a phone. She seemed reanimated, at times even happy. Of course! Since then, as many times as we've met, as many things as have happened, all happy: 22nd Party Congress, Stalin removed from the Mausoleum. And how much she made! She read me some new stanzas from *The Poem*, for some reason calling them footnotes:

> . . . Drunk with cursed dance, –
> As from a vase decorated with black figures
> I came running to an azure wave
> So splendidly bare.

In these lines about waves – the very undulating movement, the dance – undulating, and among the cursed undulation – a premonition of death:

> And why does this stream of blood
> Irritate the doe's petal?

Then she read four lines about how time flies: "But who will protect us from the horror which . . ."; then the poem "I could have made it without him" (she explained: "a dream I had in

124

Komaróvo on August 13"); then — out of her pocketbook — some note about *The Poem*: as if the petals of a flower were gradually opening. Afterward, she read some letters: one from Italy, another from London. And the third — a New Year's Day card — from Surkov.

"On the eve of my illness I received a letter from a Swedish professor who's writing a book about me. In a small Swedish university town. He informed me, he would come to talk to me. He came, and I was in the hospital. Came here. Nice man and he knew a great deal, but the most amazing thing — the blinding whiteness of his shirt. White like an angel's wing. While we had two bloody wars and a lot of blood beside the wars, all the Swedes did was wash-and-iron that shirt."

"I sent an excerpt from *The Poem* and one poem ("Aleksandr") to Moscow, to *Nash Sovremennik*. I got an answer from Sidorenko: 'You yourself must understand that it would be strange to see these poems on the pages of a Soviet magazine.' And on and on wishing me a happy New Year and creative success in the future . . ."

"Hold on to, for the love of God, hold on to this letter!" I begged.

"A second printing of *The Poem* came out in New York. With a long article by Filippov. Everything was fine, but the end worried me: he wrote I was a Russian George Sand . . . She was fat, small, wore slacks, and each of her lovers was more famous than the last . . . Before they called me a Russian Sappho, I liked that much more . . . Some things, of course, Filippov garbled. He assumes, for example, that the poet who shoots himself in *The Poem* is Count Vasilii Komarovskii. (He hung himself in Tsarskoe.) Well, now I'll just put 'Vs' in the epigraph from Kniazev and that one symbol will clarify everything."

"Tell Kornei Ivanovich to write about *The Poem*. He's the only one that remembers that time. He can latch it on to whatever, even one of his articles."

I replied: "But only excerpts of *The Poem* have been released. How can anyone write about it?"

"Doesn't matter. He can write about the excerpts."

(I thought to myself that while *The Poem* was out only in bits and pieces, no one could even formulate an impression. What's worse: one could formulate a false impression. It all seemed to be leading toward masquarade and Hoffmaniana. I know no other work which when broken up into excerpts to such an extent does

125

not correspond with itself. Its entire charm: the correlation between slices of memory, between that which has "rotted in the depths of mirrors," and the simultaneous ringing of the most realistic reality. Excerpts destroy the whole; that is, the correlation.)

"There'll be two kinds of footnotes in *The Poem*," said Anna Andreevna. "'From the editor,' which are all true, and 'from the author,' which are all lies."

She handed me some pages, prepared for me, with the new footnotes and corrections for my copy of *The Poem*. She'd already sent them to me with Koma Ivanov, but we had missed each other. I glanced down: instead of "a flash of gaslight" it now read "A cry: Don't!".

"I changed it because I discovered that modern-day readers don't imagine a gas lamp, but a gas stove. A kitchen. At first I made it 'the scent of a rose,' but that made it too close to 'in the square it smells of perfume.' But 'A cry: Don't!,' that's her seeing that he's taken out a gun.

"Wouldn't you agree that there is an incredible ascent of interest in poetry in Russia today? Our quartet's made it: Pasternak, me, Tsvetaeva, Mandel'shtam. A seventeen year old boy managed to get in here to ask me which of the four was the best. I told him, 'All three are really first class poets. Be happy with such wealth, and don't beat each other over the head with poems.' Soon they'll have new gods and godesses, in Leningrad and in Moscow. In Leningrad they're all praising red-headed Brodskii."

I asked her if she'd read Samoilov in *The Tarusskii Pages*.

"Yes. . . A tea-room. . . I also have my own tea-room."

And she read:

Even before the pot-bellied stove
There was a pub here.

About an alley in Tsarskii. Ends like this:

And atop the ruins of order
Is a giant cuirassier.

126

Anna Andreevna explained to me that the giant cuirassier is tsar Aleksandr III.

In the intonation and vocabulary of this poem there is again some new Akhmatova and again some new Tsarskii: not Pushkin's, not Annenkov's and not Gumileev's.

I asked her to read it again.

> We drank vodka late into the night,
> And with it ate rice with raisins.

Yes, completely new.

We were quiet a while. Then Anna Andreevna said:

"I got a letter from dear Iura Annenkov. He asks permission to illustrate *The Poem*."

"Is he right for it?"

"He thinks he's right for it."

(It occurred to me: maybe so. After all Annenkov illustrated *Twelve*! Then he was a local, but now . . . how would he climb with us onto "the tower of '40?" or onto the tower of '60?)

"Reeve is having some problems," said Anna Andreevna as though she had read my thoughts about Blok. "He didn't understand: with us, one can't write about *Twelve* — it's a failure. He did. Everyone was angry and hurt."

"But Anna Andreevna, the point here isn't only of the official viewpoint," I said. "The point is that *Twelve* wasn't a failure at all."

"Of course! *Retribution* — now that was a failure. A splendid, enormous failure!"

She asked me to hand her her robe from the chair, for a long time felt around with swollen feet for her shoes, straightened up and leaned heavily on my arm. We went into the hall. Again the divine smell of pine. The Christmas tree is already lit — red and green little bulbs — electricity instead of the beloved candles of mine and Liusha's childhood. Regardless, it smells like childhood because it smells like pine. Some nurses sit quietly chatting against the walls, and some patients in grey robes.

We sat on a separate little couch, and I took from my bag a blanket, some tangerines and some crushed nuts; Anna Andreevna told me that, besides Admoni and Silman, she had been taken care of here by a remarkable woman:

"She's a mathematician; Sofia Kovalevskaia is nothing next to her — Ladyzhenskaia. She brought me food, spoon-fed me, even washed the dishes herself. She lives nearby."

I congratulated Anna Andreevna on Leva's dissertation, told her — on behalf of Oksman — that Konrad considers him a great scholar.

"That great scholar hasn't visited me in the hospital once over the course of three months," said Anna Andreevna, darkening. "Forget about him, about Lev. He's a sick man. They hurt his spirit over there. They suggested, 'Your mother's so famous, she just has to say the word and you'll be home.'"

I was struck dumb.

"He won't acknowledge my illness: 'You've always been ill, even in youth. It's one big sham.'"

Calming down a bit, she announced:

"In honor of the New Year, I've begun putting together a new book in my head. It'll be called *The Last Flowers*. Two sections. The epigraph for the first will be 'The Flight of Time':

What's this war, what's this noise? — their end is near.
Their sentence is almost passed.
But who will protect us from the horror, which
Was once called the flight of time.

She was tired of talking. I gathered the sweets, walked her to her ward and helped her take off the robe. She tossed off the shoes and laid down. I tidied up the nightstand and excused myself. Going down the stairs, I thought, out of habit, "How can I leave her this way?"

The blizzard had calmed down. Quiet twilight surrounding the quiet corps. And everywhere, paths through the illuminated pink snowdrifts. Walking to the tram, I remembered about "Sofia" — that's what I forgot to tell Anna Andreevna!

*Translated by Natasha Yefimov*

128

Ludmila Shtern

# INERADICABLE

Peter Volkin stood in the middle of the communal kitchen and, puffing out his cheeks, inquisitively searched the shelves. He couldn't find one single redeemable bottle.

"Where did they hide them, damn them?" — Peter irritatedly asked space.

Space kept silent. So did time because his neighbor's alarm clock with its missing minute hand did not remind the people of apartment 6 at the 17th crossing of Pirogov St. that life was short and fleeting. Peter rubbed his swollen nose which was the color of lilacs in May and became very pensive. The problem of relieving hangover stood before him in all its terrible urgency. It goes without saying that he had no money and not the least hope of getting any.

"Beige boots." His saving grace flashed then immediately fizzled. Yesterday he had given them to Sergei, the boiler-room superintendant, in exchange for half a quart.

"That resentful tightwad Prokoshka could've just as well parted with a whole quart." Peter gritted his teeth.

He returned to his room, opened the closet, and his eyes came face to face with his one and only suit. The Romanian half-wool gazed back at Volkin with mute reproach.

"Relax, " said ˌPeter Volkin "I promised not to swap you for a shot and I won't. I swore to my sister that I'd be buried in you." This phrase which seemed innocent at first glance had a hidden prophetic meaning unnoticed by Peter Volkin.

"But I have every right to put you on," he said suddenly with indignation, pulling up his trousers, putting on his jacket, reversing the lapels to hide his lack of dress shirt and his dirty undershirt. Then he put his feet into his house slippers and went out into the street.

It was 9:15 AM in the world. The neighborhood grocer had

129

already opened. Inside and outside of it passions raged. On this May morning the epicenter was in the meat department. Finnish chickens and ducks were being sold there. The birds of passage were looking smart and well dressed in brilliant cellophane packages with golden labels. Around, the waves of anger and sorrow tired and quieted. Being apathetic to imported or domestic birds, Peter forced his way to the wine department. There it was dark and cool, like a cathedral. But Peter knew that in about a half an hour the priestess Nina Sinukhina would show up. With a magic hand she would touch the switch and the shelves of vodka, wine and cognac would light up, reflecting in the mirrors with green, red and yellow fire. Peter cast an affectionate glance at the "little ones," made himself at home at the end of the counter, and froze, intending to wait. Lifelong experience whispered to him that if the last evening in the Sinukhina family went well, then she, having lightly rebuked him, would give out a bottle of Cat's Eye "Peppered" or "Lemon" on credit. It had happened before.

But this morning turned out to be a bit fateful for Peter. Sinukhina, having shown up at exactly 11:13, didn't want either to smile or to show simple human compassion.

"Get out, damned drunk," she greeted Volkin "Get your whole self out of here, or I'll call the police."

The police was the last men with whom Volkin wanted to meet. Their meetings always carried too much of an official character. Peter sulked, mumbled a few inane death threats, and went out onto the street.

The usually scant Leningrad sun shone brightly this morning. The pale sky was free of storms and clouds. Plekhanov street tenderly and easily took Peter into its embrace, somehow saying: "Live, Volkin, in your own pleasure." However, no kind of thought out plan of life took shape in Volkin's head.

He dragged himself to Majorov Street, the main government highway. For example, once a week the black Chaikas go by carrying famous guests from the airport to their secret residencies. Peter had seen their procession many times. Marshall Tito, General

DeGaulle, Prime Minister Nehru, and the Shah of Iran with the first of wives. . . .

This morning Majorov Prospect looked empty and dull. These political stars had fallen long ago. Some were at home while others were out visiting far from the residence of Peter Volkin. At the four corners of Plekhanov and Majorov, four lines were spread out. One was for numbers at the pay clinic; another to redeem bottles; the third for oranges from Morocco; and the fourth, who knows for what?! It could be for beef, sausages, Indian cristal goblets, or Czechoslovakian pantyhose. For the experienced mind, such lines are a real boon. It's like an equation with three unknowns: X, Y, Z. X = What is for sale?; Y = Do I need it?; and Z = Will they have enough for me?

Peter Volkin didn't see the slightest hope of a happy outcome to this morning and became seriously depressed . . . And suddenly he saw a dog, a white Spitz–Pomeranian with a tail like an autumn chrysanthemum. The dog was tied to a street light and was obviously bored. Upon seeing Volkin the spitz wagged his chrysanthemum with delight.

"Hell, you bandit mug." Peter was touched. "You're melancholy it seems?"

The spitz whined complaining about fate.

"I know what you mean," Peter continued the conversation, "If you're not lucky, you're not. Join with me, Barbos, in happy company . . ."

He untied the dog, wound the leash in his fist, and started towards his home. At this very moment, Sophia Yanuarovna Shelter, a literary translator of Spanish and Portugese, came out of his gate. She was not young, not happy, and torn apart by the internal and external contradictions of life.

Having noticed Volkin, Yanuarovna automatically backed off and averted her eyes. A meeting with Peter never promised anything good. To the contrary, the meetings were a gloomy color in the spectrum of negative emotions. When drunk, he threw out insults with ethnic coloring. When sober, he would whimper and beg for money. And so, Sophyan (an abbreviation of Sophia Yanuarovna) took a step back and closed her eyes in hopes that when she raised her eyelids, this "foul type" would disappear from her field of vision. Completely different feelings enveloped Peter Volkin upon seeing the translator. He

131

experienced a momentary wicked happiness, the happiness of a man who had found the answer in the mail to an unsolvable problem. And it so happened that two weeks ago Sophia's dog was run over by a car. It was a red-haired spaniel named Rawling. Sophia was in such convulsions that her neighbors called for an ambulance two times. They were afraid that she would become paralyzed. The general opinion was that it was simply a shame to mourn so over a lousy dog . . .

"Good morning, Sophyan," Peter said ingraciously. "Look, see what I've got."

"Goodness, what a charm! Where did you get such a beauty? Did you buy it?"

"You're kidding . . ," said Peter in his habitul language. "With what?! They gave it to me at work as a bonus."

The whole wide world, with the exception of naive Sophia, knew that it had been three months since Volkin had been kicked out of his last place of employment, and he had twice been brought in for bummery and moperism.

"Boy, what a nice boss you have, Peter Ivanovich! This dog has an excellent pedigree. Very rare spitz-pomeranian!"

"Here you can buy it. I'll sell him cheap. Three rubels."

"God help you! The dog is worth much more. . . besides, it's immoral to sell a grown dog . . . It'd be the same as selling your friend."

"What, what?" Volkin couldn't comprehend.

"I can't, young lad, you understand . . . I get so attached to animals."

Sophyan put a hand to her chest, her eyes dampened, and she sobbed.

"If, Heaven forbid, something happens to it . . . I simply couldn't live through a second such loss."

"You won't take care of it, then? Then to Hell with you!" Peter took offense, "I'll make a hat out of it! My ears freeze in the winter."

"What! That's sadistic! You shouldn't even talk that way in jest."

"What do I need her for?"

Insiduous Volkin kicked the dog in the side with all his might. The spitz pomeranian squealed, and at the same time, Sophia screamed:

"Give me the dog!!! You're just a scoundrel!"

132

She opened her purse with trembling hands and shoved some money at Volkin — two three-ruble bills and some small change — everything she had.

Less than an hour had passed since Peter had abandoned the grocery store, insulted and humbled. Now, reborn from the ashes, proudly raising his head, he quickly ran back to the grocery store.

The next morning, the doorbell rang in Sophia Yanuarovna's apartment. The first one to the door was the spitz-pomeranian, warning of the stranger by barking.

In the threshold stood the wife of the caretaker, Nura.

"Did ya hear what happened here at home, Sophia? Volkin, our former plumber, died. They say it was alcohol poisoning. Last month he was picked up and taken to the rehabilitation center for alcoholics and injected with antabus. The doctor, they say, warned him that if he guzzled more than half a liter in a day he would certainly die. We conducted a meeting at the propoganda center in which we decided to keep Volkin sober and not to give him money. He, you see, was drunk somewhere and died right on the street. He had no money left with which to bury him. He doesn't have a relative except one sister who went on vacation with her husband. The landlord has sent me to the apartments in order to collect money for the burial. Not every tenant is donating, and good will alone is not enough."

During Nura's monoloque, Sophia's face distorted. She began to rub her temples with her fingertips spasmodically and even banged her head on the door jamb.

"Merciful God!" Nura was frightened. "Why are you shaking? So the man died! Who doesn't? Who was he? Your husband? Your lover?"

"It's mine, my fault. I am guilty!" Mumbled Sophia fevereshly. "Why does all this torture have to befall me?"

"What torture? Calm yourself! Look, your nervous system has failed. He was a worthless bumpkin. That man was a pile of trash — a real louse."

Nura hugged Sophia tenderly around the shoulders and led her into the room.

"Let's go and have a sip of water. Don't kill yourself. You look deathly pale in the face. But if you are low on money, don't give. Buffoon! Somehow he'll be buried. He won't be thrown out on the street."

Sophia stretched out her hand to the caretaker's wife.

"Take it, Nura, the money. Take it yourself, all there is . . ."

133

Then she fell onto her bed, burying her face in the pillow.

"My goodness! With these intellectuals it won't take you long to go crazy." Nura mumbled, fumbling in her pocketbook. Finally she found a crampled five-ruble bill. "Look, I'm taking a five. I have no change. I'll drop it off later."

For two days Sophia Yanuarovna laid in bed in tears on nitro-glycerine. She was trapped by the universally known Jewish guilt complex. Directly or indirectly, she was the cause of somebody's death. She was the killer. Her imagination drew a horrifying picture: a homeless lonely man in house slippers and a beige suit lying alone on the sidewalk or even on the carriage way among the sputtering trolleys and cars. Above all he had just been alive! He thought, he loved, he suffered. And now it has all ended. Where does his soul now wander?

On the third day Sophia ventured to leave her home in order to take the dog for a walk. The spitz-pomeranian, well educated by his previous owners, was ashamed by his unesthetic behavior on the rug in Sophia's bedroom.

So, two deeply suffering creatures left the house, turned the corner at Dekabrists' street, and, nose to nose, came together with Peter Volkin ! ! ! The deceased approached them, and his appearance was terrifying, emaciated and unshaven, in white pants and a striped pajama jacket. On his left pant leg and left sleeve was printed in high style:

Ministry of Health and Welfare

USSR

Vladimir Lenin Hospital

Leningrad

The spitz barked hysterically. His Master stared, screamed loudly, and slowly sank onto the sidewalk. Peter Volkin was in time, however, to catch her and sit her down on a nearby stoop.

"And I, at this moment, dear Sophia, turned to you. I thought I'd come visit the dog and borrow one or more rubles." Peter Volkin sneezes with gusto. "See what those bastards did with me! I am afraid I'll catch the flu or even catch pleurisy and bronchitis."

Sophia Yanuarovna began a nervous tremble, her teeth chattered, and she didn't even have the strength to utter a word.

"In general, if you examine what happened to me . . . how incredibly funny," continued Volkin good naturedly. "Can you imagine, the day before yesterday, I was resting here on Plekhanova street, not bothering anyone. Some fool called for an ambulance. Some snotty medical students showed up to certify my death. To die with such people . . ." Peter Volkin burst out laughing. "Well, they transported me straight to the morgue. I will not forgive them for burning my suit. They said that I could'nt be buried in it because it looked like it had been dragged through the mud. But the prorector, the one who cuts up the dead, was away at his summer home. Without his certificate of consent from the committee, one cannot be buried. Then they wrapped me up in cold storage for twenty-four hours. The guy, the one who cuts people up, showed up this morning, took me out of there and put me on the cutting table. Suddenly he was suspicious of me. He says to me, he says, 'I had doubt because you sneezed. And stiffs neither should cough nor sneeze.' He began calling all the medical departments, hardly able to dial the telephone. Doctors came running to gather around me. In my whole life I never saw so many. In convultions they arranged themselves all around me. The main doctor came forward and said that in fact the super-cooling of an organism could allow it to come back to life although it would contract diseases in various parts . . ." Peter Volkin paused, blew his nose into his sleeve, and continued.

"And my brain could easily become diseased, and my digestion, and even . . . my privates. So he told me, 'You, Volkin, go home, but be careful, and keep an eye on yourself.' Then he ordered me to wear these hospital clothes because, I don't remember if I told you or not, my suit was burnt up . . . so, Miss Sophia Yanuarovna, be helpful and give me something for warming my soul and body. And for this — if your faucet ever leaks, or your toilet seat cracks — I am forever at your service, even if in the middle of the night, wake me."

Not lowering her exhausted eyes from Peter Volkin, and not ceasing to tremble, Sophia Yanuarovna opened her little purse and gave Volkin three rubles. Now this time it was really her absolute last.

*Translated by: Christine Winn*
*and Doug Perkins*

135

Tatiana Nikolaeva

# LENINGRAD – TBILISI

The second night Anna also slept badly. In the morning the train stopped in Tbilisi, where, if one were to believe the stories, a woman couldn't walk down the street alone: she would be bothered for sure – nor go to the movies alone – she would be bothered. She couldn't do anything alone. . .

Anna was dreaming that some dark-haired people were pulling her by the arms in different directions. She broke away from them, ran down the street, hurdles were put in front of her, she stumbled, ran on, turned the corner, went into a garden, a man jumped out from behind a bush, grabbed her, dragged her into the bushes, tearing at her clothes. Anna pushed him away in horror, ran on to find refuge in a woman's bathroom, ran in, sighed in relief, but the breath stuck in her throat – there were men seated on the toilets, beckoning to her and laughing.

Anna awoke. Her neighbors snored peacefully. The conductor was passing through the car.

The train arrived in Tbilisi at five in the morning. The city transport wasn't running yet. Anna nervously waited in line for a taxi. They had warned her that it was dangerous to take a taxi at night. But it was morning now. . . . Anna told the driver the name of the hotel where she had a reservation, and they went through the city. The whole way, Anna sat hunched up, looking at her knees. When the cab stopped at the standardized hotel building, she gave the driver a five-ruble note and to her amazement received change.

Three hours later Anna left the hotel. She was hungry, but didn't feel like going to the hotel buffet. They bothered you in hotels even in Leningrad. On the streetcar she went as far as Rustaveli Prospect. Along the flagstone-paved street grew lush, beautiful trees. Anna went to a telephone booth. The telephone didn't work. The next one didn't either. As she left the third, a man asked her "Mushaobs?" ["Does it work?"] Anna was frightened, remembered her dream and ran. Passersby turned and made incomprehensible remarks. Anna decided to get a hold of herself. She walked calmly. She found a working telephone. . . She was invited to dinner at a Georgian house at five o'clock.

At the corner of Rustaveli Prospect and the street leading to the mountain, Anna came across a store that sold sodas. "Rose, mint, cream, chocolate, tarukhin, kokhuri," Anna read the names of the syrups. Filling a glass, the woman at the counter mixed the syrup in with a small spoon. In Leningrad they didn't do it like that. In a neighboring establishment people sat at little tables eating round flat pies.

"May I eat something here?" Anna asked the waitress.

"Sit down, *genotsvale,* I'll be right with you."

After twenty minutes Anna washed down a hot pie with cheese filling with an ice-cold soda.

"What do you call this pie?"

"Khachapuri, *genotsvale.*"

Feeling slightly weak, Anna looked through the window at the strolling crowd. The men, despite the hot weather, were dressed in dark blue suits; the women wore suede skirts, multicolored knit ponchos and bare feet in "platform" sandals of multicolored leather.

\* \* \*

"Finally, you're here, come on in, my dear," Anna was greeted by the hostess of the Georgian home. "I berated myself for not inviting you right away. You could have had lunch with me and told me about things. 'Why didn't I think of it! *Vai me!* [ah me!]'"

The hostess led Anna into a study crammed with books.

"My husband will be right here, just wait a minute, my mchady are burning."

Books stood in shelves stretching to the ceiling, lay on the

137

desk, on chairs, on the couch.

The professor burst into the study. Thick-set, short, in a round white felt hat with a black cotton tassel and blue training pants. Through his netlike summer shirt thick grey hair could be seen.

"Sorry to keep you waiting. I just came from work, and had to change," he announced to Anna. And without letting his guest put in a word, he went on:

"Well, you're something to see, Anna Vyacheslavovna. . . if you don't object, I'll just call you Anna; they call me Sergo or Batono Sergo. We don't use patronymics in Georgia — that's just your Russification."

The professor spoke quickly, with a heavy accent.

"You don't know any Georgian? You'll have to learn if you want to study Kite seriously. 'Batono' means 'Mister', that's probably how your Soloukhin suggested addressing people? How did you get here, where are you staying? If you like, come stay with me. What's the news in Leningrad? Your letter made me very happy. Finally in Russia they're taking an interest in Alkhazishvili. Kite loved Russian literature. Did you read his article on Yevreinov? Yevreinov is a remarkable playwright. A superb theory of the theatre for its own sake. Why does your government not publish Yevreinov, Rozanov or Merezhkovsky, and yet they publish Gribachev and Sofronov? You're young, explain this phenomenon to me. Did you know that Kite was friends with Yevreinov? I knew Yevreinov personally. He came to see us in Georgia and wrote a remarkable play here — *The Main Thing* — about actors on the stage of life."

The professor slid onto a chair and rapidly going through the books on the shelf, found *The Main Thing*.

He wanted to show Anna something else, but his wife came into the study and asked them to come to the table.

On the table was chicken with nut sauce, beans, a white young cheese, a tray with greens, brandy, wine and mineral water. The professor's wife brought freshly baked mchady — little rolls of corn meal, which turned out to be quite flavorless. The rest of the food, though, was very spicy. Anna was told the names of the dishes, but she couldn't remember anything. They drank to her visit, to Georgia, Leningrad, Alkhazishvili, and

138

Yevreinov. Her hosts name the environs of Tbilisi that had to be seen, the museums and theatres, the names of people who had known Alkhazishvili.

"Stay in Georgia a while, learn the language," Batono Sergo advised her, "and then write a proper article, maybe even a book about Kite, and publish it in Russia. Let them know what a remarkable writer lived in Georgia. Here they don't talk about him now, because he went abroad. Your Bunin was also an emigre, and yet they publish him. Kite's friends included members of the Central Committee, but they rejected him, the time hadn't come yet, you see. No paper. But for your Gribachevs and Sofronovs there always seems to be paper," the professor said indignantly.

"Easy, Sergo, calm down, you're making trouble for yourself," his wife tried to reason with him.

"No, I won't calm down," the professor raised his voice. "What have they done to Georgia, the country of Rustaveli! And who did it? That *kinto* Stalin, whose mother was a prostitute at the Gori station!"

"Sergo, they'll put you in prison," his wife pleaded with him.

Anna didn't expect a Georgian to talk like that about Stalin. She had seen today the Stalin Quay, photos of the former leader on the windshields of cars; a large portrait of Stalin assembled from different types of wood was on display at the souvenir shop, alongside those of Yesenin and Chalyapin.

There was a ringing at the door. A tall young Georgian entered. He was in a dark blue suit, of course.

"Grigol, how lucky that you've come!" the professor greeted his guest. "Anna, mèet our Grigol, he is a writer, and knows Kite's work very well."

Grigol sat down next to Anna and began asking her the same questions she had answered for the professor an hour before. Learning that Anna had not yet seen anything in Tbilisi, Grigol offered to take her for a drive through the city at night.

"But not for too long," Anna warned him. "They close up the hotel at eleven."

"Have you been to Mtatsminda?" Grigol asked.

"No."

"Mtatsminda means 'holy mountain.' Our great people are buried there."

From the mountain more and more cars descended along the narrow backstreets to Rustaveli. There were some real traffic jams, the drivers leaned out of their cars and shouted something in Georgian.

Grigol turned onto a steep cobblestone street. Anna was able to see the store where she had drunk the soda this morning.

"That's Lagidze's store," Grigol explained. "Its proprietors know the secret of making the tastiest soda. And khachapuri there are the best in Tbilisi."

The car turned endlessly, climbing the mountain by a narrow winding road, and finally stopped at the entrance to the Pantheon. Grigol showed Anna the grave of Griboyedov, the monuments to Akakii and Ilya (as they referred to Tsereteli and Chavchavadze in Georgia, by their first names), the fresh graves of Georgian poets Georgii Leonidze and Simon Chikovani. Afterwards, smiling, Grigol led his companion to a black and white marble tombstone.

"And this is the grave of Stalin's mother, Yekaterina Dzhugashvili. Tourists from Russia come and the first thing they ask is: 'Where is Stalin's mother buried?' Even Griboyedov interests them less. They think that we have a Stalin cult in Georgia. Of course the shoemakers and the tavern-owners, the uneducated people, love Stalin. Because they don't know how much evil he brought to Georgia. But our intelligentsia hates him. I was talking to a Russian woman in Leningrad who served a ten-year term in Kolyma, and she said that the Georgians in the camp opened the Russians' eyes to Stalin. He cut down almost the entire flower of our intelligentsia."

"Unfortunately, here on Mtatsminda, along with decent people the traitors and turncoats are also buried. There, you see, next to Ilya's grave his murderer is buried. When they buried him here, even the wall was indignant and crumbled."

Anna sat with Grigol on a bench and silently looked at the roofs of Tbilisi's houses.

"Do you believe in God?" Grigol suddenly asked.

"I do," Anna answered.

"Do you know Vladimir Solovyov?"

140

The conversation turned to Russian philosophers. Vying, they named Berdyaev, Shestov, Ern, Shpet, Florensky, Lossky. . . .

"By the way, did you know Florensky was from Tbilisi? and Lossky, and Ern as well. In my opinion, it's no accident," said Grigol.

Anna didn't answer. It was getting dark. With dizzying speed Grigol drove the car to the bottom of the holy mountain. Anna was frightened, but didn't ask him to slow down.

Anna went to sleep happy.


\* \* \*


For breakfast Anna went to Lagidze's store. This time she descended a marble stairway to a basement where they served khachapuri in the form of a cheese tart. Over the melted cheese floated egg yolk. A piece of cold butter lay next to it. You had to use a fork and knife, so that the yolk didn't run out onto the plate. Anna tried to imitate the movements of her neighbors, who skillfully broke off small pieces of pastry from the edge and dipped them into the appetizing heart.

After breakfast Anna went to see an old resident of Tbilisi, whose home, according to Batono Sergo, Alkhazishvili had often visited. Straying through the alleys and dead-ends of the old city, she entered the courtyard of a five-story stone building. On each floor wooden glassed-in verandas had been built. High above the ground beautiful imported linen was drying on lines. The spiral outer staircase, decorated with marvelous ironwork, made the courtyard unusual. Anna wanted to go up the spiral staircase, but wash basins and cardboard boxes blocked the passage. By the shabby interior staircase she went up to the second floor. There were no numbers on the apartments. On a guess Anna rang at one of the three doors. It was opened by a stately grey-haired woman.

"Excuse me, does Vera Semenovna live here?"

The woman smiled: "That's me, come in, please." Seating Anna on the couch, Vera Semenovna disappeared, but quickly returned, carrying before her a tray with a jar of yogurt, a sugar-bowl and cups.

"Try the matsone. They bring it to our courtyard every morning from the mountains. In the meantime I'll made coffee."

Learning that Anna was studying Alkazishvili, Vera Semenovna was overjoyed.

"He was a brilliant man. Even in those hungry times in 1919 he dressed like a dandy, with a red carnation in his buttonhole at all times of the year. He argued with such passion that I understood everything, even though we never studied Georgian in school. All the friends of our family, Georgians, spoke Russian then. And even I, though I was born in Tbilisi and have lived here all my life, never learned the language. Many were in love with Kite. Now his speeches seem bombastic to me, but in those years Kite was regarded as a prophet by us girl students. . . . They were interesting years. At that time a whole *beau monde* came together in Tbilisi. Everyone was there: Cherepin, Yevreinov, Kamensky. And everyone came to our house. My father was a journalist, and my sister and I organized literary Saturdays.

\* \* \*

Anna wandered for hours around the city, which she no longer feared. She tried to read the signs painted in beautiful Georgian letters. But sometimes the letters were stylized in capitals and she wasn't able to make them out. She stopped by the bazaar. On the first floor they were selling vegetables. In enormous bunches. The names disturbed the ear: kindza, tsitsmata, reikhan, ombala, and so on and so on. There were crowds of people in the passages between counters. More men than women. They were bargaining. Shouting. The sellers extolled their merchandise. The greens were sprinkled with water. The drops glistened. A variety of pickled products. Dark cherry-colored cabbage, fermenting in coarse lumps. Small Jojoli flowers floating in brine. On the second floor were fruits. Apples, pears, green and black figs. Plums – tkemali, alycha, greengage. Pomegranates, persimmons, chestnuts. Tempting little sausages of Churkhchela: the thin ones were Cahetian and the thick ones Imeritian. A variety of spices. Bright orange garlands of saffron. Cheeses. Young tender ones. Old ripe ones, porous, strong-smelling. The best was a Gouda that was a little like Roquefort. The pale little carcasses of suckling pigs. Live chickens and turkeys.

"How much are the apples?"

"A ruble thirty."

The buyer walked away.

"Don't go away, dear, you can have them for a ruble."

"Eighty copecks."

"Ninety."

"I'm buying a lot, give them to me for eighty."

"If you buy five kilos it's a deal."

Anna bought a Churkhchela. She had been told that the Churkhchela was bad at the bazaar. You had to go to Cahetia to buy a good one. But she couldn't restrain herself. To make Churkhchela they trampled grapes with their feet, mixed the grape juice with flour, and boiled a pelamush. They threaded nuts onto string and dipped it into the vat full of pelamush. Then they dried it in the sun. They dipped again, dried again. Just like that. Sometimes the Churkhchela was too sweet or too mealy, sometimes it melted in your mouth, and once in a while it had an unusually winey smell.

Leaving the bazaar, Anna went up to the square, came to a pharmacy in which the medicines prepared to order had old-fashioned pointed paper labels stuck to them with black rubber and an old sign said "No Loitering," turned on Leselidze street and slowly descended towards the Kura. She passed a snack-bar in whose windows hung cages with canaries. She stopped in front of the window of a photographic studio. She looked at photographs in enamel painted in bright colors. She was especially charmed by the picture of "Love and Power," which showed a half-naked rosy girl embracing a reddish lion. Passing by the synagogue, she turned toward the Sion Cathedral, went down to the church and, throwing her head back, met the gaze of Christ contemplating the passersby from the cupola. Beams of light from the little carved windows illuminated the images of the saints. She looked into a second-hand shop, where they sold old silver belts and enormous bison horns. Leselidze street ended at the Kura. On the opposite bank, clinging by some miracle to the cliff, were little multicolored wooden houses. No doubt it was terrifying to live there. You could lean out the window and plunge into the turbid river. One could reach the Orbelian sulfur baths, go up the narrow lane into the Botanical Garden or cross the bridge to the Metekhsky Castle and from there, along the "Wine Slope," arrive at Avlabar. But most of all Anna loved to return along Kapyaev street, high above the Kura, which was so narrow that a car couldn't pass along it. Sometimes she had to duck to avoid wet linen hanging on a line across the street. From Kapyaev street there was a view of Maidan, the old Eastern district of Tbilisi, made famous by Knut Hamsun and Iosif Grishashvili, the district where Niko Pirosmani lived. Returning to the Rustaveli, Anna went to the post office to pick up her mail. She wrote the replies right there. She ate khachapuri at Logidze's or pancakes in the Nargizi cafe, where cooks from the Metropol' in Leningrad worked. Then, after stopping into the Kashvetsky church to look at the voluptuous Georgian madonna painted by Lado Gudiashvili, she went to the library. She looked through the old newspapers for articles by Alkazishvili, and copied letter by letter the Georgian texts.

Almost every evening Anna met people who had known Kite, and from bits of information, like a mosaic, she put together a picture of her idol.

*Translated by Alan Shaw*

# Bella Akhmadulina

# THE MANY DOGS AND THE DOG

## Excerpt from novella

Again noticing his hand wounded by the wasp, Shelaputov came to: the wrist hurt and itched, the palm embraced the back of The Dog's head.

Leaning on The Dog's Head, Shelaputov caught sight of the great multiplicity of sea with its silvery scum and of the garden deceived by the blinding semblance of scorching heat and again desirous of flowering and decking itself out. On the shore, Ingurka, weakening and snurling dully, eluded her inevitable fate. Now without pride and potting on of airs, she shook off first this, then that embrace. Red was dispersing the lot of them with his thin, authoritative bark. Another little pack played not far off: the girl Ketevan was laughing and running away from Gigo.

The Dog's nape rose under Shelaputov's hand, and Shelaputov's shoulderblades tensed. He turned around and glimpsed Pyrkin, who was getting ready to go to the city. He did not at all know this no-sort-of man and was struck by the strength of his gaze, the trajectory of which was distinctly outlined against the light, pierced Shelaputov's crown, exploded where the scrap of chain was, and managed to cause contusions all about. He was sending his gaze voluptuously and was not able to break off this activety, but Shelaputov also looked at Pyrkin potently.

Bound for the bus station, Pyrkin grabbed the stones of the mountains together with houses and kitchen gardens and flung them at the foreign evil spirits of the dogs and children, at the whole fork-tongued Proustian bunch of pigs aiming to escape hard labor and devour the feijoa.

"Here's what, brother," said Shelaputov. "Go on, do not yield to

Red the farewell smile of our sad sunset. And I'll go to town and ask those who understand: what is a man to do, when he wants to depart with his Dog."

The beast set out, downcast. Shelaputov did not bother to watch how he stood there with his head down, while Red, jumping up and falling back chewed the air around his lion's paws superficially, with Ingurka, in his support, wrinkling her nose, her upper lip quivering, hostile thin points bated, to the approval of all the secondary participants.

He didn't bother to watch how Gigo caught the laughing Ketevan. Indeed, can light be caught, a gold column of undefined dust? – but there it was caught and, for a joke, held above the surf, and the surf, for a joke, feigned taking it. But she fell back and back, again flowed out through his fingers, glittered freely in the distance – the equal of a ray, indistinguishable from the rest of the sun.

An ancient bus with a tarpaulin top shook over the potholes until the contents – various appearances, nationalities, subspecies, and breeds – were thoroughly blended by the end of the trip, equally spotted, wrinkled and unified – exept for Pyrkin and Shelaputov. Look what a city, what an Athenian-white and colonnaded one, with a crown of structure on the peak of the mountain; oh, not the Parthenon – after all, I don't make any pretenses – but a restaurant where they are out of shashlik – but what a city beloved by Shelaputov. Here it comes, a rich outlander, possessor of pompous exccesses of palms, rhododendrons, and eucalypti, gypsum close by and basalt afar off. An azure, acrid, hairy city lusting after a sovereign and inaccessible sister: oh, how it would like to crumple her fleur d'orange, oh Nice, oh!

Shelaputov headed for the Cook office, walking along as always with his hands wound as tight as would go behind his back, grabbing his right hand firmly in his left. Bewitched Pyrkin went along behind him for a time, trustingly inclining his head to the side for thinking over that peculiarity of his walk, and he even said something encouraging to him, but Shelaputov again forgot to notice him.

Cook not being present, the associates to whom drifted this time without satisfaction through the ins and outs of the line explained to him fastidiously what it was necessary for someone to do if he wanted to depart with his Dog. There wasn't enough room for all that in the time alotted to Shelaputov; there really wasn't enough for

146

the muzzle, repair of the broken chain, and a separate cage for the traveler. Tired and faded, Shelaputov set out along the embankment, burdened by the unmitigated magnitude of the sky, the mountains and scurrying life. The sea was absent whitishly and right beyond the parapet began nothing. The natural born twin of the human crowd that loiters, trades, obtains women or some other prey, he was again entirely alone and leant only on the weaving together of his hands behind his back.

Having taken a seat in a seaside coffee house, Shelaputov took to watching how the Greek Aleko, elegant, wiry, blackishly grey, handled a brazier with burning hot sand. No prattling motion − just the short flight of a strong elbow, the sparkle askant of a capacious eye that foresaw the black brew's every new need, that grinned at the cafe fortunetellers: not for him answers from an overturned cup, he was sharper than the all-knowing grounds.

Shelaputov remembered nothing, knew everything that momentary − move it. Chink! − hour for getting things together, graves − there, Aleko − here.

Sensing Shelaputov, Aleko blazed at him lovingly with his eye: wait a bit, I am coming, don't grieve, and prosper forever and ever. There is a look between man and man for which it is worth living in this meffable world with its shining sea and fragile, gigantic magnolia holding up its porcelain cup of light. Getting the better of the usual batch of copper in the grounds, Aleko came up, with a light touch of his palm greeting Shelaputov's shoulder. About The Dog he said:

"Go to this address and make a deal with the conductor. He'll be here tommorrow evening, the day after tomorrow you and your Dog will go off with him."

Then he extinguished his eyes and asked:

"Have you seen Ketevan?"

"Go there, Aleko," answered Shelaputov, gazing at him distinctly. "Don't delay, go today."

Aleko looked at the expanse of day, at Greece in the distance, briefly played the end of some music on the table with his fingers, and said with a brash grin.

"I'm an old, poor Greek from a coffee house. And she − you know yourself what she is. I'll be going back to my place. Farewell, brother."

But how beautiful you are, Aleko, in you there is everything. You have seen everything under the sun, exept the higher whiteness – the beloved homeland of your ancient and valorous blood. The Nike of Samothrace is with you! Let us close our lids and commence to think that sea resembles sea, as one drop of water another. And what gleams white on the mountain top so harmoniously? Not a temple in honor of the beginning and the end of a shashlik but a thought without miscalculation, beauty without fault: The Parthenon.

Shelaputov embraced a wrecked column, attending to the rough marble with his forehead. Below, the Acropolis was pulled up tight farther down and farther out the port of Piraeus bustled with dignity, quite far off, beyond the sea's mirage, twelve men indistinguishable one from the other, entered the coffee house. What sort were they? Probably negotiators successful in trading of musk, ginger, and slaves, celebrating the usual deal. But where had Shelaputov seen them before? The lovesick serving girl was moving the tables, lugging bottles and victuals. Victoria is theirs, no doubt, but do they actually have too few drachmas to win over the hand that greases the features of their faces, that raises their stomachs' sick fat that is dangerous to their happy life? Br-r, however, how they look.

"Get a move on, Greek!" But he's coming with a cup and a copper vessel, irreproachably stately, like Lysippus's fabrications, gaily glancing at them with all-knowing eyes.

"Here, Greek, drink up!"

He takes the glass with a polite bow, fixedly examines the liquid, where something teems and multiglies, laughs with bold fresh teeth and says lighheartedly:

"Your wine is dirty."

He says nothing more, but they, raving, hear:

"Your wine is dirty, thievish curs. A curse on him who drinks it voluntarily; sorrow to him who bends his neck to it. This one's a Greek, that one's somebody else, but you are nobody from nowhere; you've got many holdings but no homeland, because all that is yours is foreign, taken away from others."

Thus he is silent, places the glass on the table and goes back to his place along the great Panathenaic Way, through the Propylaia, the Erechitheion toward the Parthenon.

Farewell.

There was some sort of directive or invitation for Shelaputov, which he forgot but which he responded to. Stepping briskly and officiously along, sincerely and fleetingly stroking the living wool of palms on the way, he went along darkening streets toward the winking lighthouse of an unknown goal. Here is the youthful house with the crumbling plaster, the necessary floor, door, the disinterested bell with wires not linked to electricity. He knocked, waited, and went in.

The gloom of the room was crammed with a smell that made it hard to breathe and to move on forward – otherwise how would Shelaputov have sniffed out the thickness of the fragrant stink?

Everywhere, in pots and boxes, quivered and coiled balletically unearthly, perversely beautiful flowers.

Face to their bell–mouths, back to Shelaputov, stood Pyrkin, trembling, fussing in rapture over his imminent good fortune.

There his hand fell and a howl of triumph and pain resounded.

Having rested and cooled to the tiresome, enticing flora, Pyrkin turned away from the puzzlingly peering, unquenchable plants, caught sight of Shelaputov and shouted at him with dignity:

"I'm on pension! I raise orchids!"

"Hmm–hmm." Shelaputov shrugged his shoulders silently. "That's nice."

They headed for the bus and then home: in front, Shelaputov, closing his hands together at his back, behind, Pyrkin, looking after the back of his head.

Shelaputov climbed up to his place, left the door open, and waited.

There – a cautious ringing in the garden and up the stairs. Shelaputov embraced The Dog's head, pressed his face against it and backed off;

– Eat.

That night, Red showed up for a short while: had a bite, hastily licked Shelaputov, squeakily bellowed at The Dog, lay unconscious on his side for a moment, then dashed off.

A grand tender star addressed itself to Shelaputov persistently, but with what? All life long, man tries to divine the meaning of that persistent link, and only in the moment following the last moment does the blinding answer dawn on him, that perfect knowledge which is given to no one to share with another.

Shelaputov woke up, because the dog got up, militarily flexing his fur and his muscles, gurgling in the depths of his throat.

"Stay!" said Shelaputov, and gave the door a shove.

Something poured off the stairs, crackled in the bushes, and abated. Without fear or interest, Shelaputov looked into the darkness. The dog came out anyway and stood next to him: a shot and another and another blazed at random across the heavens' star. An echo and another and another pushed off from the mountains, banged heads with the cry of the bad–shot–of–a–failure:

"All Frenchmen are kikes! They do the cattleya! Hide fugitives! Steal feijoa!"

"Can't you sleep?" said Shelaputov, "Oh, yeah, you are afraid of dying in your sleep. Be careful, I know a good lullabye."

In the morning, Shelaputov, stiff with cold, tarried in bed, but then, he had nothing to do the while. Out the open door, he caught sight of modest, lacy dandyishness – the earth's primordial delight, which he attempted to elude on the iron handrails wound round with grapevines, on the dead little bodies of the persimmons wounded–by–frost, northern whiteness glistened icily. Scorching her tiny fingers on it, Madame Odetta, in a most charming padded jacket, climbed the stairs. She had to stop on the threshold in confusion:

"Oh! I beg your pardon: you aren't dressed yet and you aren't even up."

The gallant, well–bred Shelaputov was in fact dressed in all his clothes and got up forthwith.

Madame Odetta viewed him pensively with her sky blue moistness beautifully arranged around vigilant black pupils that knew the thought that was difficult for her to express, something like:

"The reason that prompts me to clarify things between us lies in my past." (The blueness increased and infused the cheeks.) "You see, Pyrkin, devoid of polish and excess education, has a subtlety of his own. His strange trips to the city. . . ." (The moisture dried up, but the pupils tried tenaciously to read Shelaputov.) "They are essentially a journey in my direction, an overcoming of hostile symbols that hinder his power over me. He's terribly jealous of my dead husband – and with reason." (Sky blue streams.) "But I want to speak about something else." (The whisper and triumph of black over blue.) "Be careful. He never sleeps so as not to die – he sees everything. Pyrkin is a danger to you."

"But who is he – Pyrkin?" asked Shelaputov, getting absolutely muddled, suddenly terribly agitated, beginning to speak confusedly and as if not sober: "Pyrkin – that is not here, that is something

150

quite other. I swear to you that you simply don't know! There, next to the station, is a hill edged with pines and a lovely church with rather fancy cupolas, one completely gold, and there's a field below and houses on the other shore. So there, if you go toward the top of the cemetery and, not from below but to one side, from the side of the road, you'll be certain to see a forgotten grave above which there isn't anything, only a pole sticking out of the ground with an inscription on it: 'PYRKIN!' Imagine? What ineradicable character, what vitality! To go to the station for vodka, to push your cap down over crazy eyes, to sit in that very cemetery, on a holiday, amid the colored eggshells, to feel in your relieved body a joyous foredoom to a fight, to yell a song until a tear of invincible sorrow wheezes in your throat, ultimately to perish foolishly, and to send this happy vertical cry outside: 'PYRKIN!'"

"You're lying!" called out an invisible, unearthly Pyrkin of the same name. "That's another someone or other, a thief, a drunkard, a loafer with three convictions! Who slept all the time, red-eyed most likely – up and died, the fool!"

No one stood in door-opening anymore, screening the thawed, unbearably shining garden, while Shelaputov kept looking at the sacred hill so belived by, so unavoidable for, him.

Having awaited the hour when the sun, which had done all possible for the warming up of these gardens, had begun to the impartial care of other gardens and peoples, Shelaputov came out through the wicket gate to the shore and got stuck in the wet pebbles. The sea was already training the slow-witted earth with boxing on the ears and a fist in the teeth, but as befitted her, nobody understood a thing, as before.

Out of nobody's boxtree, tearing free out of somebody's enclosure, Gigo emerged lazily in a striped sweater, once more without occupation and intention. Far away, behind, covering her face with the whole of her long hand refracted in a beautiful wrist dipped in coming, soapy infinity, came the girl Ketevan, not looking golden.

The sun, before departing into the clouds irrevocably, beat the tambourine of orange fur, and Red crossed his forepaws on a woolfishly goatlike, darkly light neck. A structure was erected out of him and Ingurka and froze. The massed assemblage played out its role, sitting around, looking on. Far from the frozen circle dance stood the big old dog, watching.

"Forget it!" said Shelaputov to him. "Let's go."

Ahead was the point of the cliff on the sloping shore; someone else had turned back to look, when forbidden — Shelaputov ran his palm over the thin spine — lion fur took off from the caress, and a wave of wrinkles passed over the scars and marks.

He said: "Wait for me here, and tomorrow we'll leave" — and without looking back, went off to find the conductor.

The place was not too distant, but Shelaputov went far into the depth of quickly-thickening night, staring now into the dead end of a thicket, now at the precipice in road above a cold trout stream. The sky did not give away in anything its assumed presence, and Shelaputov, discrete from the universe, languished inside the stony, airless dark as in an exitless elevator.

There was a glimpse of deliverance, and the sky was bared at once, with its stars and impeccable moon, whose ripening Shelaputov had lost from view behind long clouds, and he was now struck by the sight if it and by its significance. Right in front of him, on an illuminated hillock, stood an arm of the law armed to the teeth and sobbing violently. Waiting out the first pity and respect for the man's grief, Shelaputov, ashamed, turned to him nevertheless for instructions — he, not suppressing his lunar tears, explained with a movement of his hand: where.

Women in black from head to toe met Shelaputov on the porch and took him into a house. He did manage to admire a mournful nobility of their dress that was independent of variegated present time, noting only later how with a light, silky crackle his heart burst, and this was not painful but mint-sweet. An old man, the head of the house, and other men stood around a table, besprinkling bread with wine. And they gave Shelaputov wine and bread. The old man said:

"You drink, too, to Aleko." He poured a little wine on some bread and drank the rest up.

How cool in the chest, what sharp wine, how beautifully blended with its taste was  its familiar, blatantly ozonous aftertaste. Was it actually retsina? No, it was a local black brew, while retsina looks golden in the light and sets the teeth on edge and delights the mouth with its gold. But all the same — hail, Aleko. We always die earlier than they, their knife keeps pace with our back, but their death will be more terrible because great is their fear before it. How pitiful people are, in essence. And do they not value their poor life so voraciously because it will undoubtedly not have a continuation and no one will weep over them from grief and not for profit?

Shelaputov drank another glass, though he anxiously knew that it was time for him to go: he fancied he saw the star shake thrice and go out.

*Translated by H. William Tjalsma*

Irina Ratushinskaia

# THE LITTLE GRAY BOOK

Now I ask you, who would have seen it coming? If your day had started out as Ivan Andreevich's had, would you have figured it out? And that's assuming you know as much about life as Ivan Andreevich — unlikely! Just try getting young people these days to listen, or to pay any mind at all to what they're told.

So! Sneering already, are you? Well, just wipe that sneer off your face and listen when you're spoken to. I don't have to tell this story, you know.

As I was saying, Ivan Andreevich was a WW II vet, in other words, a veteran of the Second World War. Just between you and me, he hadn't really been in combat; he'd been in charge of a food warehouse in Tashkent. But at the end of the war he'd pulled a few strings and managed to get a piece of paper that indirectly implied that he had been in combat. So when the time came for discount rates and special privileges, Ivan Andreevich had everything in order, and, you'll agree, with good reason.

If you think that a person with privileges has it any easier than you, then there's no sense even explaining. But I'd like to see you try running around some morning instead of Ivan Andreevich.

154

First thing, of course, Ivan Andreevich set off for the ration center (Aniuta had asked for oranges) and insisted that he be allowed to choose his own fruit. Unless you show those people who's boss, they'll eat you alive. He also ordered a Kiev torte for the next day, not because it was a special occasion, just to maintain his prestige. If you still don't know, I'll explain. In Kiev a Kiev torte is a perquisite torte, one you can't buy anywhere, not to mention order in advance, and available only to the deserving few. And don't think we don't see the look on your face when you run into someone on the street carrying a Kiev torte in a string bag. And all you've got are sour grapes!

Next, Ivan Andreevich went down to the railroad station and bought tickets to Moscow for Sasha and Masha, though, of course, he shouldn't have. Let them stand in that snail parade for a couple of hours only to find out that there aren't any sleeper tickets, then they'll appreciate their grandfather, the punks. Too much of a good thing, but what are you going to do? Your heart's not made of stone! After all, what does it cost him: he bought them as soon as he got there, without having to stand in line, and nobody made a peep. He didn't even have to show his little gray book. Too bad, though. Showing your book can be enjoyable, provided, of course, you do it right. First you let some milksop make a scene and demand his rights, and then (take that!) you whip it out. After that the whole line will make him pay for his happy childhood. He'll be lucky to get away with both legs intact.

You think Ivan Andreevich went home after that? Then you tell me who went to the pharmacy with the special prescription card? Just being able to get the right medicine made it worth the effort. What with things the way they are these days it's downright amazing there's anything left for veterans. People are getting spoiled and once in a while you've got to tighten a few screws. Nerves, by the way, aren't made of steel. Elderly people ought to be taken care of. Oh you'll take care of them all right!

Here's an example for you: when Ivan Andreevich walked out of the drugstore, he saw they were selling frozen Yugoslavian fruit and, sure enough, a fight had already broken out. Some bitch (no spring chicken either, though she acted just like one of those modern hussies!) started laying into Ivan Andreevich about how she'd been made a widow at twenty by the same war — as if that meant an old veteran should be deprived of his lawful rights! How do you like that? And you think it was easy putting her in her place? Lucky for Ivan Andreevich he hit his mark with the first shot; he told her it remained to be seen whether her husband hadn't really deserted to the enemy; there seemed to be an awful lot of so-called innocent victims around these days. At which point she started bawling and left, thank God.

It was one of those days, though (isn't it the truth?) not terribly out of the ordinary. So how in the world was Ivan Andreevich supposed to know what was coming when he got on the bus and tapped that lug sitting in the nearest seat and showed him his little book? Do you know what that lug did? Got up and offered his seat?

Oh no! Instead, he looked up at Ivan Andreevich and shouted for the whole bus to hear:

"You're a veteran? Well, I'm a madman!"

Then he started growling, the bastard, and grabbed the book in his teeth. The young hussy sitting next to him all of a sudden turned out to be his wife and started hanging all over him and carping about how the man's just sitting here quietly minding his own business when – of all people – they go after him! Could have asked someone healthy to get up, but no, and now how was she going to calm him down, she'd spent the whole morning . . . and so on and so on. . . . At which point the madman lunged at Ivan Andreevich and snatched his little book. His wife (we know those wives!) dragged him to the exit. Ivan Andreevich first thought of following them off to get his little book back, but when the madman started snarling "come on, come on," and yanked Ivan Andreevich by the sleeve, Ivan Andreevich preferred to free himself and to stay on the bus.

Go ahead, smile, smile! You, of course, know better what he should have done. Everybody has twenty-twenty hindsight. Two hours later Ivan Andreevich also figured out what he should have done, but that was two hours later; at the time all he did was cry out "How disgusting!" though no one on the bus picked up on it.

What was done was done, so the next day Ivan Andreevich set off to see Piotr Nikolaevich at the Veteran's Committee. Piotr Nikolaevich wasn't in his office. At his desk sat a younger man, one of those administrative assistant types, looking like he owned the place. Ivan Andreevich had no choice but to ask him when Piotr Nikolaevich would be in.

"Why do you need to know?" he answered the question with a question.

"Listen," Ivan Andreevich said coldly, "it's none of your

business.  What are you doing here anyway?  What's your name?"

"I, citizen, am Comrade Artamonov's replacement," the guy said sweetly and to Ivan Andreevich's horror, showed him a little gray veteran's book with his picture pasted inside.  This threw Ivan Andreevich for a total loop and he just stood and stared at the upstart.  Forty, at most!  But, on the other hand, he did have that little book. . . .

"And who, may I ask, are you?" the ornery comrade persisted.

"You see," Ivan Andreevich mumbled, "I lost my veteran's book yesterday, and I'm in your files, . . . you can check.  Pavliushin's the name.  I'd like to get a new one."

"There must be some mistake," the other grinned sweetly.  "I know for certain you're not in our files."

"What do you mean?  You didn't even look, and you've never seen me before!  How do you know?" Ivan Andreevich protested, fully realizing that it wouldn't help.

"I told you in plain Russian, citizen, there's no card for you, there never was, and I don't have to check.  I just know!  Can you show me any proof?"

"I told you I lost it . . .," Ivan Andreevich said dejectedly, and there the discussion ended.  He walked outside and set off, deaf and blind to the world around him.

You're snickering again, aren't you?  I should have known.  Just try and get a little sympathy from you!  I shouldn't have told you the whole story in the first place.

All right, fine, but I want to see you forty years from now!

Irina Ratushinskaya

# A MISUNDERSTANDING

Of course, everyone loved Ol' Sania. How he'd become part of the group no one quite knew, probably through the Mozhaevs. In any case, he had shown up with them a couple of times, and later he just came by his sharpnosed, repressed, haphazardly clad self.

His introversion didn't bother anybody, because it wasn't contagious. Just the opposite – in Ol' Sania's presence people felt witty and articulate.

"Ah-hah!" everyone would shout. "Ol' Sania's arrived! How are you, Ol' Sania?"

And, though he himself never gave much of an answer, the question would instantly fire speculation on the state of Ol' Sania's affairs. The most intriguing theory would then be elaborated and embellished by the chorus, giving rise to one of those free and easy conversations that wind steadily on their own, demanding no special effort, to the end of the evening.

Ol' Sania would promptly fade into the background, sit down in his favorite spot at the west end of the couch, and just sit there, grimacing and rocking back and forth, until the time came to leave. Gradually, everyone grew accustomed to Ol' Sania's complete and total uselessness and to his absent-minded reactions to questions, and eventually everyone came to cherish his quirks: without Ol' Sania something was missing, and everybody was always thoroughly delighted by his arrival.

Once, though, Ol' Sania violated tradition. It was at the Mozhaevs', where the group had gathered to view slides of Africa. Jokes about possible forgeries quickly gave way to the subject of aliens in general, and to Jonathan Swift in particular, when suddenly the lights failed. Of course, a dash was made for the fuse box, but it turned out that the power was down throughout the entire building and, consequently, there was nothing to do but wait. That's when Ol' Sania started squirming and wriggling, turned himself into a kerosene lamp, and then just stood there and burned.

Naturally, had Ruben or the host pulled a stunt like that, everyone would have raved, and this simply marvelous little incident would have outshone even last year's when Yevseich, flashing his handmade cufflinks, had produced eight cards in a row – all sixes. But more depends on style than on substance, and so Ol' Sania's metamorphosis produced absolutely no thunder, indeed, was sort of glossed over; a few people didn't even realize where the lamp had come from. Someone trimmed the wick, the conversation resumed, and then the lights came on again.

Yet the incident did not pass entirely unnoticed, and after that, whenever something was desperately needed, Ol' Sania was called to the rescue. Ol' Sania never refused, serving, respectively, as a cassette deck, an ice cream maker, and when Tat'iana was finishing her dissertation, spending his entire vacation in the shape of a typewriter.

After that he only rarely made it to his favorite spot on the couch.

"Ol' Sania," shouts would greet him as he unwound his scarf in the doorway, "where have you been? It's already twenty minutes into the second segment! Give us a picture, ol' buddy!"

And, without a murmur, Ol' Sania would turn into a cordless color television set. He had lost a little weight and now spent his idle moments perched in some corner, and something vaguely birdlike had come over him, but nothing you could put your finger on, really.

Around about then spring arrived, that hectic, vitamin-deficient time of the year, and everyone got buried in work. The get-togethers grew fewer; everyone was too tired. Not that the jokes and stories had run dry, they just weren't gushing, and no new flood could be expected until September, when everyone would come back from vacation, garrulous and tanned, with a fresh load of surprises and stories to tell. Nevertheless, when Lioshka's collection of poems was published, telephones rang, projects were dropped, and the whole crew appeared, bellowing up the stairwell.

Though he was too late for an autographed copy, Ol' Sania also came, but his entrance went unnoticed in the gales of laughter over Ruben's parody of Lioshka's poetry, delivered complete with Lioshka's convulsive intonation. The evening lasted longer than ever before; at 1:30 a.m. a card game got underway, and out came the cigarettes again, this time until dawn. Towards morning tempermental Kiriusha was scribbling a new scorecard when he broke the last remaining pencil. All the pens had run dry, and no one could find anything else to write with. That's when Ol' Sania was brought into the act: without a word, he turned himself into a plastic pencil sharpener shaped like a football with a hole on the side.

Ol' Sania was remembered a second time just as the party was breaking up. He was still lying on the sticky glass, amid pencil shavings and drinking glass stains.

"Hey, Sania, ol' boy, sun's up!"

But the plastic football didn't budge, and there was no shy Ol' Sania in the corner either, only the pendulum of the tabletop clock marking out its predictable beat. That's when people started to worry and to plead with Ol' Sania.

"Come on, old man, wake up. What's the matter, your feelings hurt?" softly cooed Yevseich. "Sania, sweetie, why are you being so difficult?" beckoned Aniuta in her platinum voice. But to no avail. Finally, it was decided that Ol' Sania had pulled a fast one, that he'd planted the pencil sharpener and taken off when no one was looking. Everyone promised to let him have it next time for playing such practical jokes, then left, almost reassured. Really ought to give him a call, but it turned out that no one remembered either his phone or his address.

Ol' Sania never did show up again, which put a damper on the next gathering, but with time the whole idiotic incident was gradually forgotten. Especially since the pencil sharpener had vanished, too.

*Translated by Diane Nemec Ignashev*

# BIOGRAPHICAL NOTES

AKHMADULINA, Bella (b. 1937). The most popular Soviet poetess of the last two decades, author of many collections of verse. She established her reputation in the same years (the early 1960's) as Yevtushenko, Voznesensky and Aksyonov. In 1979 she contributed to the almanac *Metropol'*, published in the West, for which she was attacked in the Soviet press. (The published excerpt is taken from her short novel, published in *Metropol'*, with the kind permission of Ardis publishers.) Currently she frequently travels abroad, giving poetry readings at universities and to emigres.

AKHMATOVA, (Gorenko) Anna Andreevna (1889-1966). Great Russian poetess of the 20th century. In the period from 1912 to 1922 she published six collections of verse. After this she was practically unable to publish new verse in the USSR. She published only translations, which were also her only livelihood. Her first husband, the poet Nikolai Gumilyov, was shot in 1921, and their son, the well-known historian L. N. Gumilyov, spent many years in camps and in exile. In 1946 Akhmatova's work was the object of a literary pogrom by A. Zhdanov. The first major collection of her verse appeared in the West in the years 1965-66. Many dissertations, studies and reminiscences have been published about her, and every year new ones appear. Among them are the fascinating memoirs of the poet Anatoly Naiman, who was her literary secretary in 1960-66.

BARANSKAYA, Nataliia Vladimirovna. Born in 1908 in St. Petersburg into a physician's family. Graduated in the Faculty of History and Ethnology of Moscow University. Her first literary productions were published by the journal *Novy Mir* in 1968. Subsequently she appeared in *Zvezda* and *Yunost'*, and published the collection of stories *Otritsatel'naia Zhizel'* (1977). Characteristic of her work is a constant interest in the mundane matters of life, an accuracy of detail and a highly professional style.

CHUKOVSKAYA, Lidiya Korneevna (b. 1907). Writer, translator, editor, essayist. Daughter of the famous writer Kornei Chukovsky. In 1940 she wrote the short novel *Sofya Petrovna*, describing the Stalin terror, which was published in the West in 1966. In the sixties and seventies she was active in the human rights movement, and came out in support of A. Sinyavsky, Yu. Daniel and A. Solzhenitsyn, for which in 1974 she was expelled from the Soviet Writers' Union (membership restored in 1988). The published excerpt was taken from the book *Zapiski ob Anne Akhmatovoi (Notes on Anna Akhmatova)*, vol. 2 (Paris, YMCA Press, 1980).

GINZBURG, (Aksyonova) Evgeniya Semenovna (1906-1977). Worked as a history teacher at Kazan University; wife of the prominent communist leader Pavel Aksyonov and mother of the future writer Vasily Aksyonov, she was also a party member. In 1937 she was arrested for "terrorist activity." After 18 years in camps, prisons and exile, E. Ginzburg, freed and rehabilitated, told of her fate in the book *Krutoi marshrut (Steep Road)*, which became widely known and appreciated among the Soviet intelligentsia, but was banned from publication. In 1967 her first book *Steep Road* was published abroad, became a best seller, and was immediately translated into many languages (in English under the title *Whithin the Whirlwind*). Only in 1977 did Evgeniya Ginzburg decide to make public her second book, which also made a great impression. In the USSR *Steep Road* first appeared in 1988 (in the journal *Soviet Latvia.*)

GREKOVA, I. (Ventsel' Elena Sergeevna). Born in 1907 in Tallin, graduated from the Mathematics Faculty of Leningrad University (1929), professor, doctor of engineering science. (The pseudonym IGREKOVA reflects her mathematical profession.) Success and recognition came to the writer from her stories "Za prokhodnoi" ("Inside the Gates"), "Damskii master" ("The Hairdresser"), and "Na ispytaniiakh" ("At the Testing Site") published in *Novy Mir* in the 1960's. Author of several books of prose, she lives in Moscow.

ZERNOVA, (Zevina, married name Serman) Ruf' Aleksandrovna. Born in 1919 in Tiraspol, finished secondary school in Odessa, in 1947 graduated from the Spanish Department of Leningrad University. In 1938-39 worked as a translator for the Republican Army during the Spanish Civil War. In 1949 she was arrested for antisoviet propaganda (conversations with friends on the growing antisemitism in the Soviet Union). Released in 1954 by amnesty.

Began publishing in 1955. Published several collections of stories, appeared in *Yunost', Ogonek, Zvezda,* and elsewhere. Emigrated in 1976, lives in Israel. In the West she is active as a publicist and translator, has published two books of stories and sketches.

MANDELSTAM, Nadezhda Yakovlevna (1899-1980). Wife of the poet Osip Mandelstam, author of the famous reminiscences of him and the literary milieu of the years between the 1920's and the 1960's. After O. Mandelstam's arrest in 1938 Nadezhda Mandelstam lived in different provincial cities, working at odd jobs and teaching English. Many of Mandelstam's verses were preserved only because she hid his manuscripts throughout these years, and learned many by heart and kept them in her memory. *Hope Against Hope*, which appeared in the West in 1970 and 1973, caused a furor, and was translated into many languages. Joseph Brodsky has written some heartfelt articles on N. Mandelstam and her book.

NIKOLAEVA, T. (pseudonym). Leningrad philologist. The publishers have no other information about this author. The published excerpt is taken from her short novel *Moscow - Tbilisi,* which came through samizdat channels. It is published without the knowledge or consent of the author.

RACHKO, (Yefimova) Marina Mikhailovna. Born in Leningrad in 1937, graduated from the Polytechnical Institute there. Journalist, poet, translator, editor. She has written for Leningrad radio and television, published in *Yunost'*, *Avrora*, *Koster* and elsewhere. Emigrated with her family in 1978. In America worked for Ardis, afterwards for Hermitage. Published in *Posev, GEO,* the newspapers *Novoe Russkoe Slovo* and *Novy Amerikanets* and elsewhere. Her book *Cherez ne mogu (Overcome 'I can't')* was published by Hermitage in 1990. The published excerpt appeared in *Posev* no. 3 from 1981.

RATUSHINSKAYA, Irina Borisovna. Born in 1954, graduated in 1978 from the Physics Faculty of Kiev University. Unpublished in the USSR. In 1982 she was arrested for human rights and literary activities and sentenced to 7 years of camps and 5 years of exile. As a result of worldwide protests the Soviet authorities released her at the end of 1986 and allowed her to leave with her husband for the West. Prior to her coming to America and Europe several collections of verse had appeared. Translations have been published in journals and newspapers in dozens of countries. She lives in

England. Two stories included in this anthology were first published in the collection *Tale of Three Heads* (Hermitage, 1986).

SHTERN, Lyudmila Yakovlevna. Unpublished in the USSR, but closely connected with the circle of Leningrad literateurs including D. Bobyshev, J. Brodsky, S. Dovlatov, I. Efimov, Y. Gordin, A. Kushner, V. Maramzin, A. Naiman, E. Rein, B. Vakhtin, and many others. Took part in the preparation of the five-volume collected works of J. Brodsky for samizdat. Emigrated in 1975, lives in the USA. Has published two collections of stories (1980 and 1984), appeared in *Kontinent, Vremya i My,* and in the newspapers *Novoe Russkoe Slovo, Novy Amerikanets* and elsewhere. Many of Shtern's stories have appeared in American journals (*Short Stories, Vogue),* and one of her short novels was published separately in Italian.

TSVETAEVA, (married name Efron) Marina Ivanovna (1892-1941). Great Russian poetess of the 20th century. Daughter of the founder and director of the Moscow Museum of Fine Arts I. V. Tsvetaev. From 1922 to 1939 she lived in emigration (Czechoslovakia, France). In the USSR her works were banned until 1965. Since then collections of verse and prose have sporadically appeared, but still very selectively. The published excerpt is taken from her sketch (essay) "My Jobs," first published in the emigre journal *Sovremennye Zapiski* in 1925 (No. 26).

Spring flood

Moscow rooftops

The latest news

Time to throw off a few pounds

Off on a ski trip

Street artists in Leningrad

The cruiser *Aurora* in Leningrad

A line for *kvas*

Next door neighbors

Roses come to Siberia from afar

The opera house in Irkutsk

An old house on the banks of the Baikal

A village on the banks of the Baikal

Rug cleaning

173

Arbat street in Moscow

Private market

Red Square in Moscow

## OTHER BOOKS IN ENGLISH FROM HERMITAGE

**You can also order a Russian
edition of this book:**
*ROSSIIA GLAZAMI ZHENSHCHIN* 8.50
(Please note that the English
text on every page is the precise
translation of the Russian text on
the corresponding page of the
Russian edition.)

РОССИЯ
ГЛАЗАМИ
ЖЕНЩИН

20% disc. with the order of 3 books or more.
$2.00 postage and handling.
Send orders to Hermitage,
P.O.Box 410, Tenafly, N.J. 07670, U.S.A.